BATMAN AND THE OUTSIDERS

The CHRYSALIS

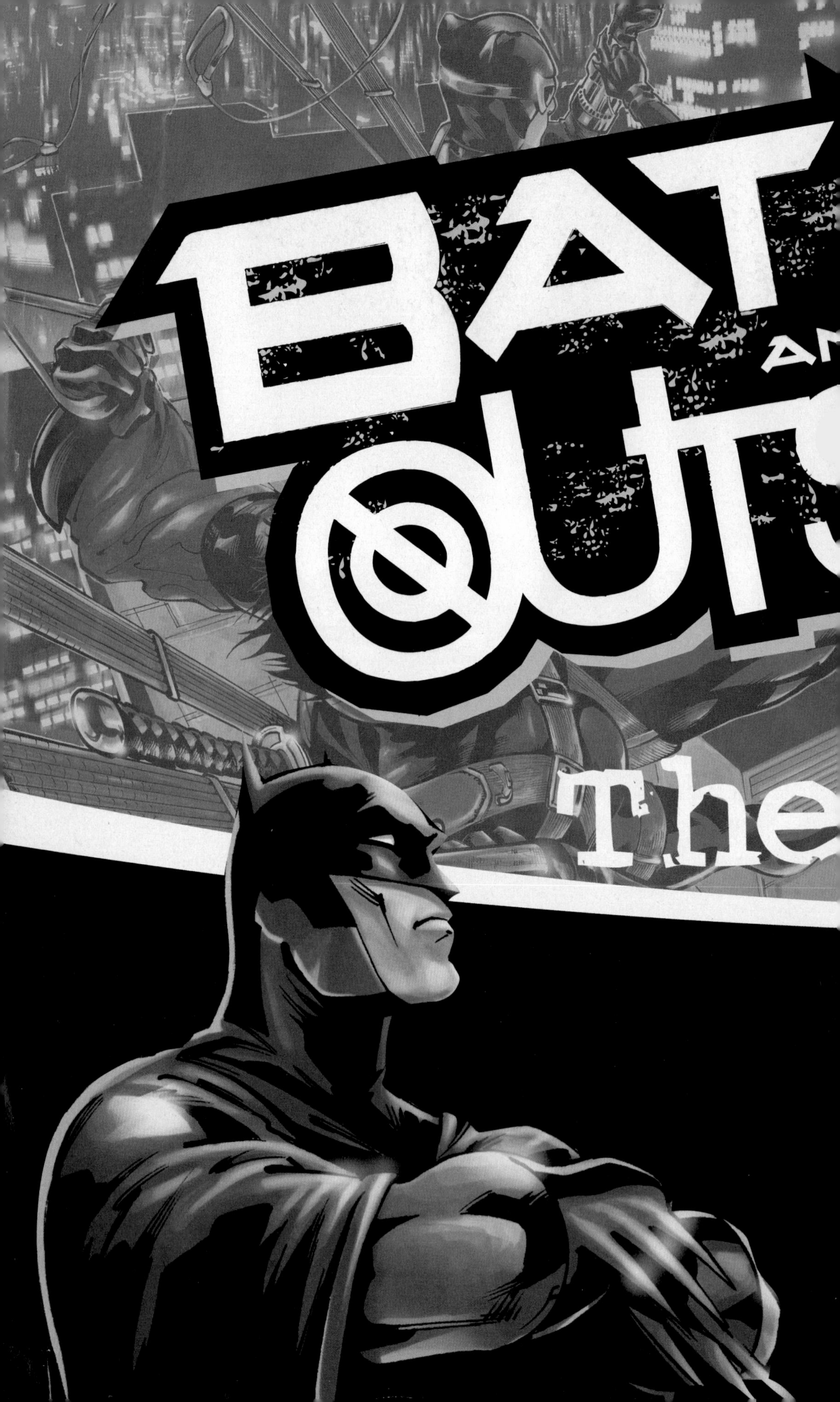

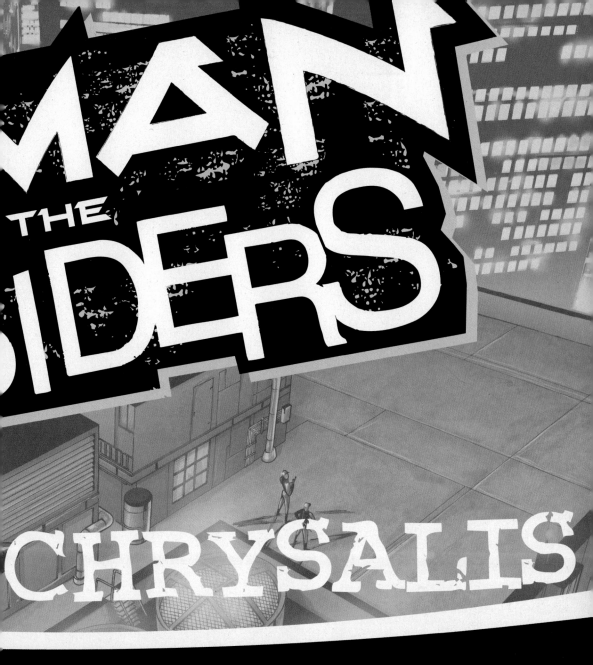

CHRYSALIS

WRITTEN BY
CHUCK DIXON

PENCILS BY
JULIAN LOPEZ
CARLOS RODRIGUEZ

INKS BY
BIT

COLORS BY
MARTA MARTINEZ
JAVIER MENA

LETTERED BY
TRAVIS LANHAM
KEN LOPEZ
NICK J. NAPOLITANO
STEVE WANDS

ORIGINAL SERIES COVERS BY
DOUG BRAITHWAITE
RYAN SOOK
ERIC BATTLE
ART THIBERT

BATMAN CREATED BY BOB KANE

Cover art by Doug Braithwaite.
Cover color by Brian Reber.
Publication design by Joseph DiStefano.

BATMAN AND THE OUTSIDERS: THE CHRYSALIS

DC Comics, 1700 Broadway, New York, NY 10019
A Warner Bros. Entertainment Company
Printed in Canada. First Printing.

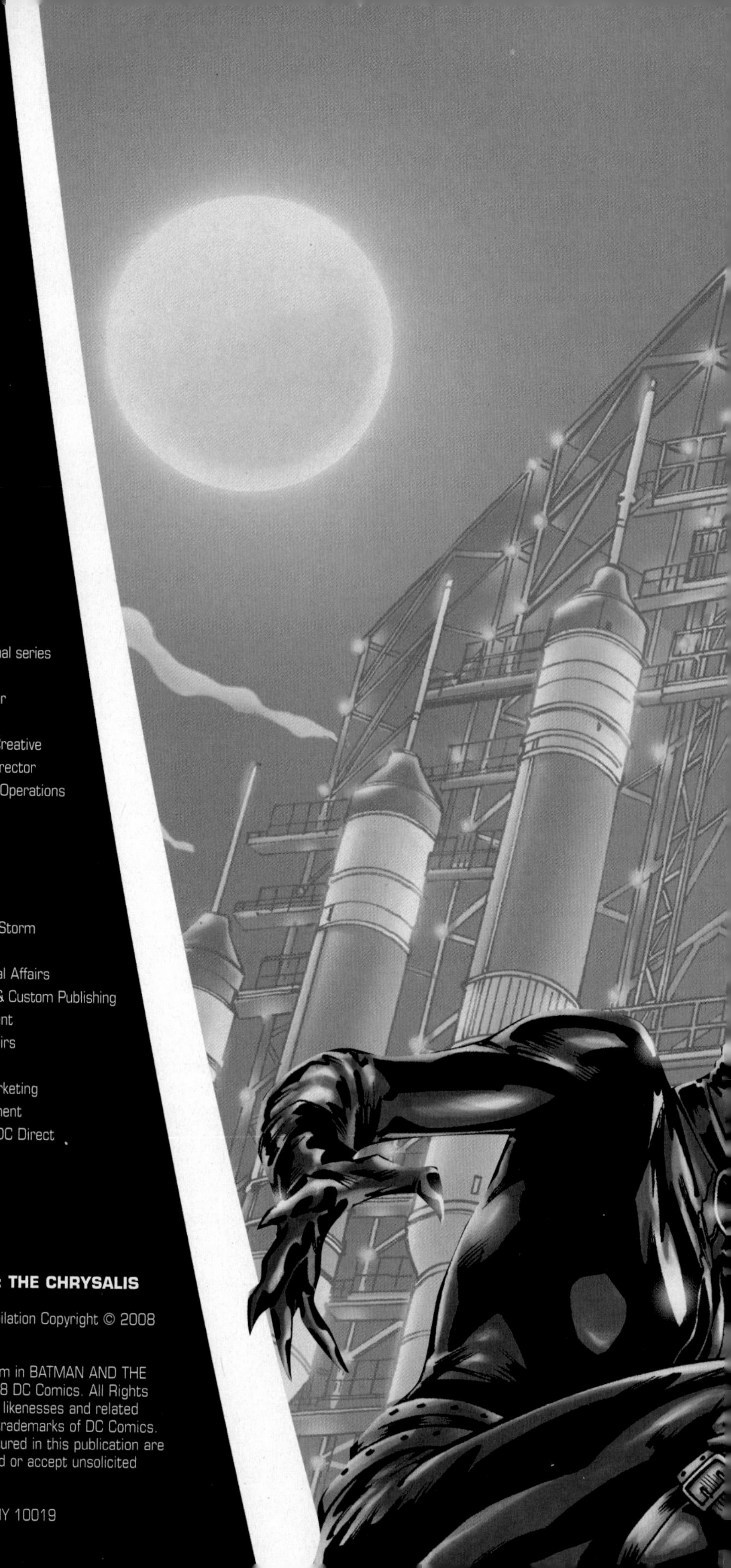

Contents

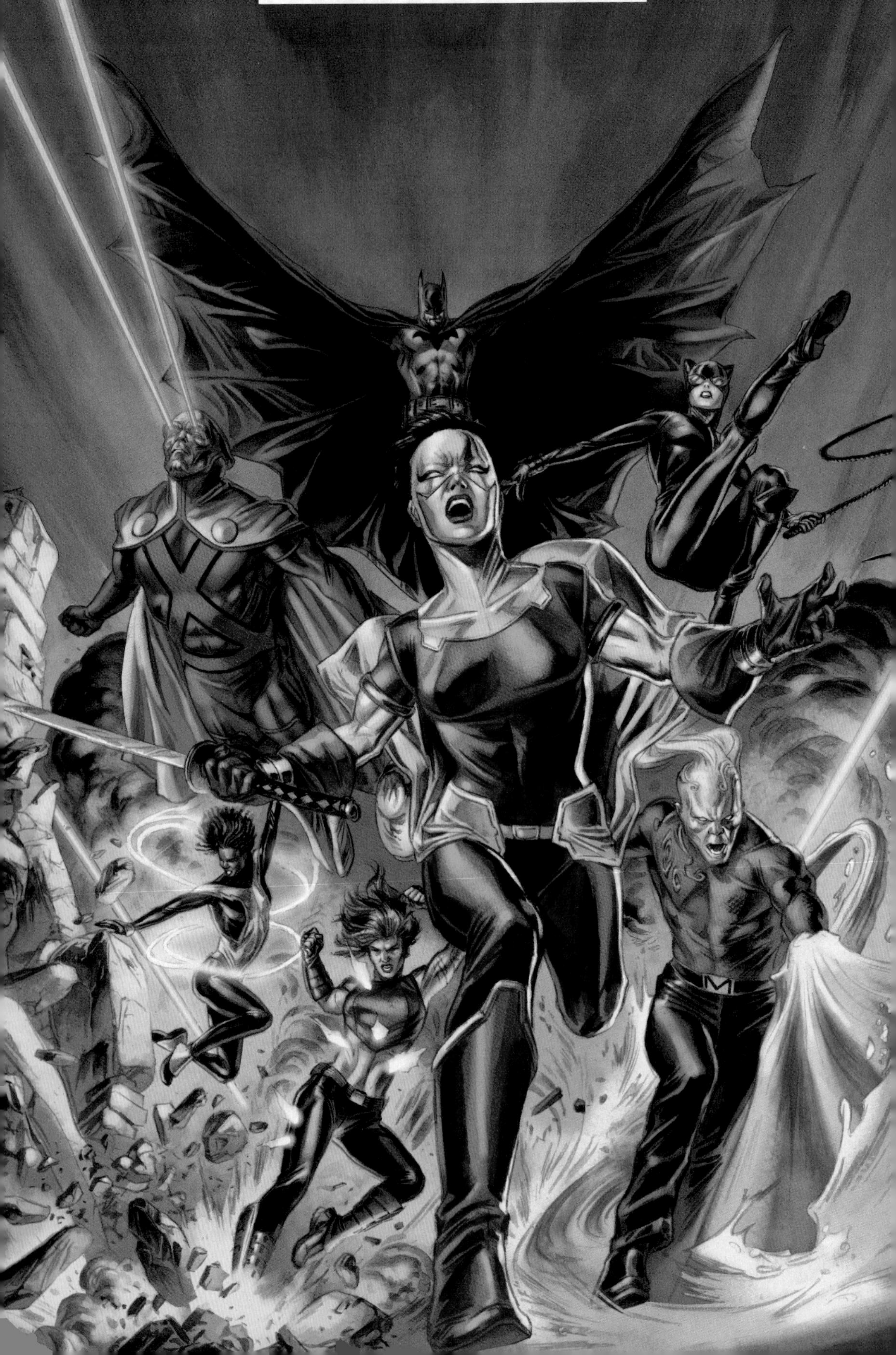
M

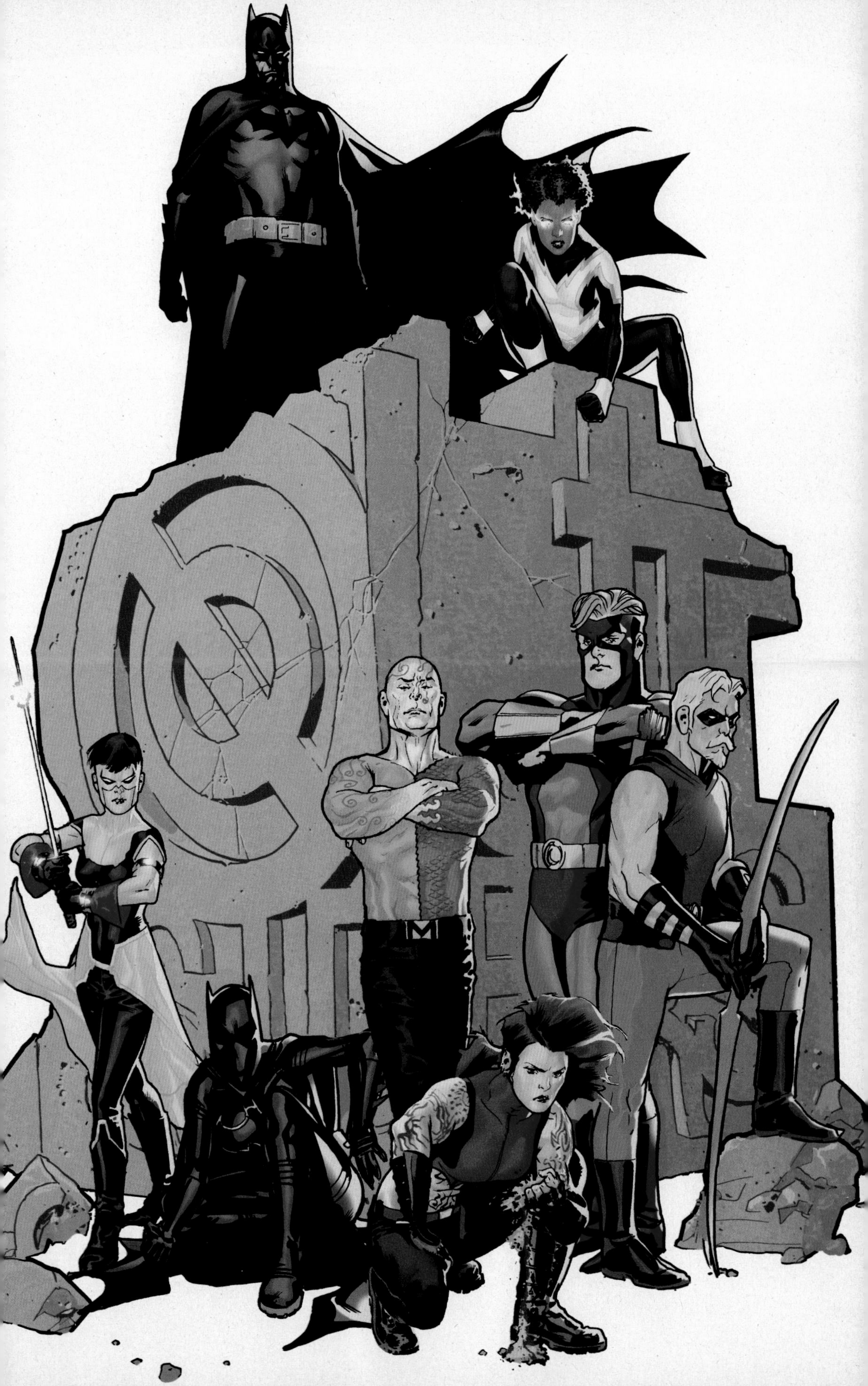

part ONE

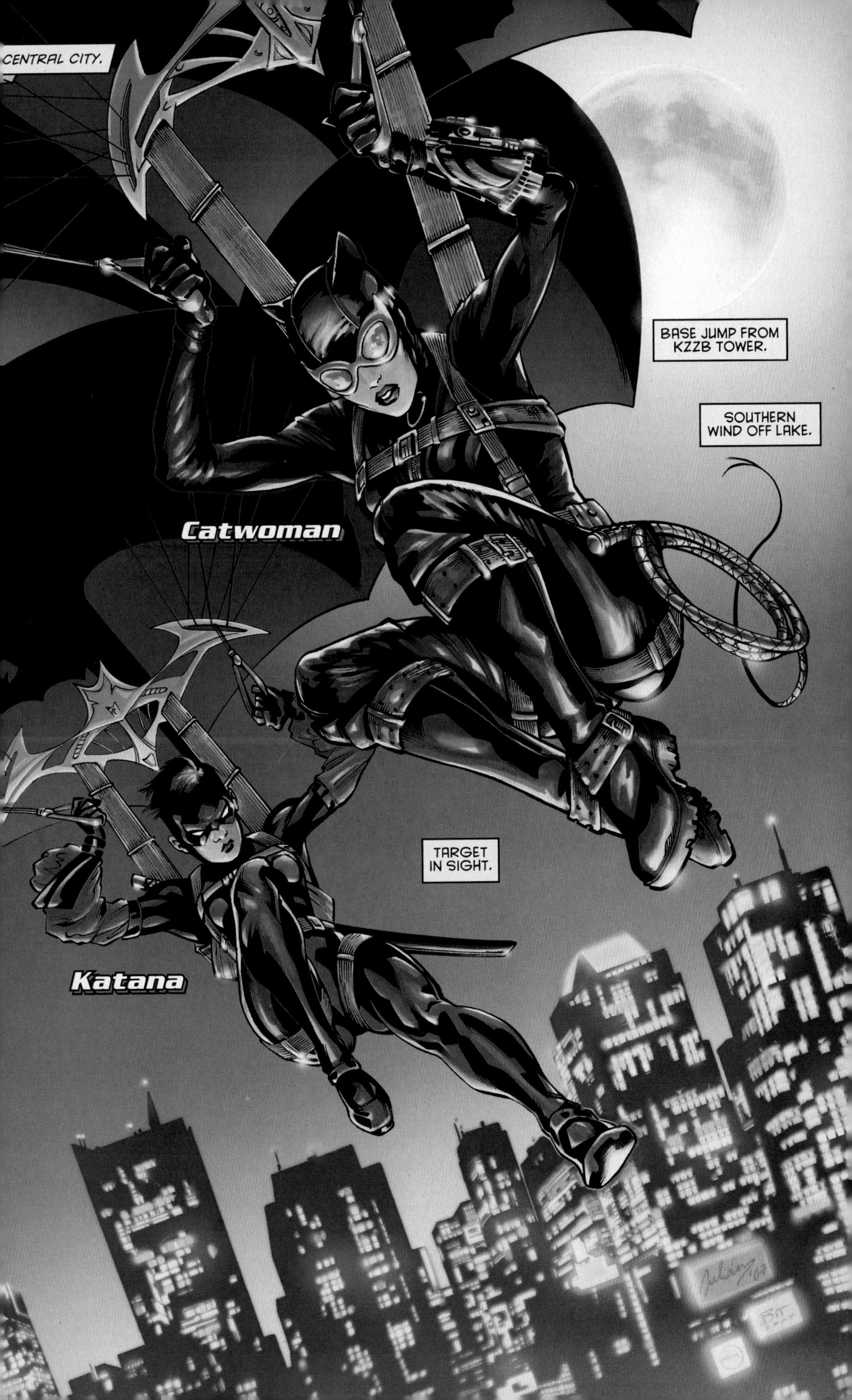
CENTRAL CITY.
BASE JUMP FROM KZZB TOWER.
SOUTHERN WIND OFF LAKE.
Catwoman
TARGET IN SIGHT.
Katana

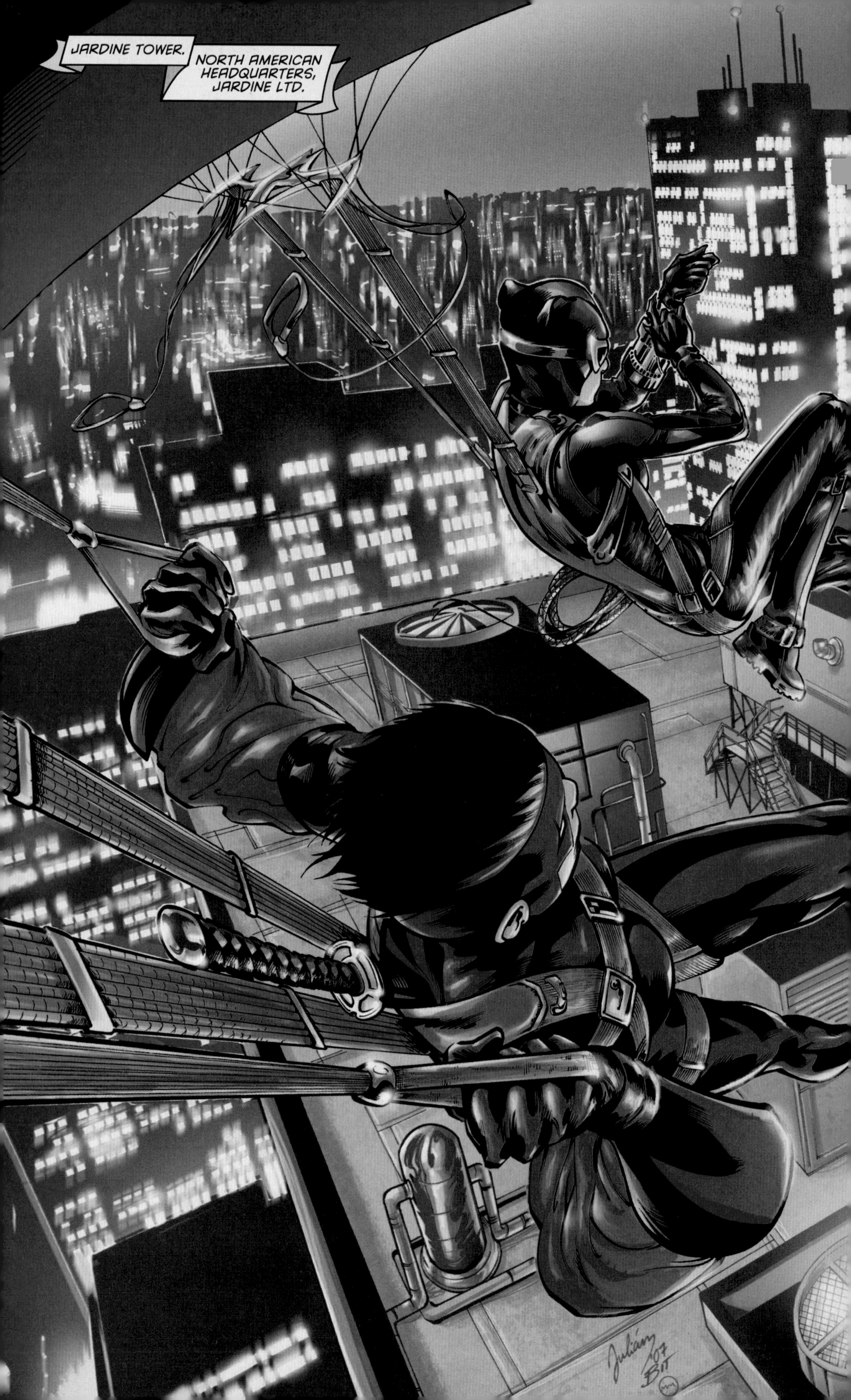
JARDINE TOWER.
NORTH AMERICAN HEADQUARTERS, JARDINE LTD.

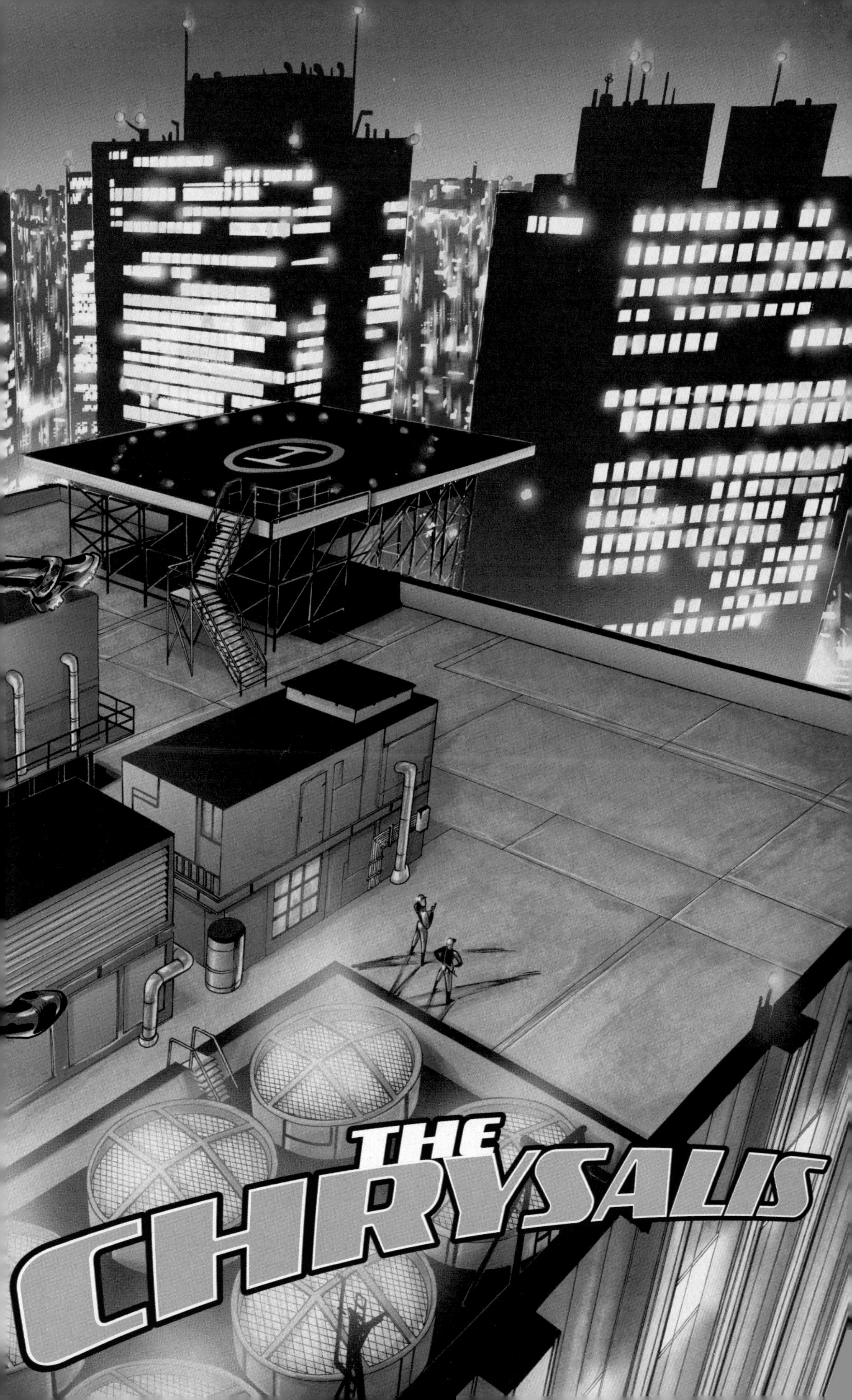
THE CHRYSALIS

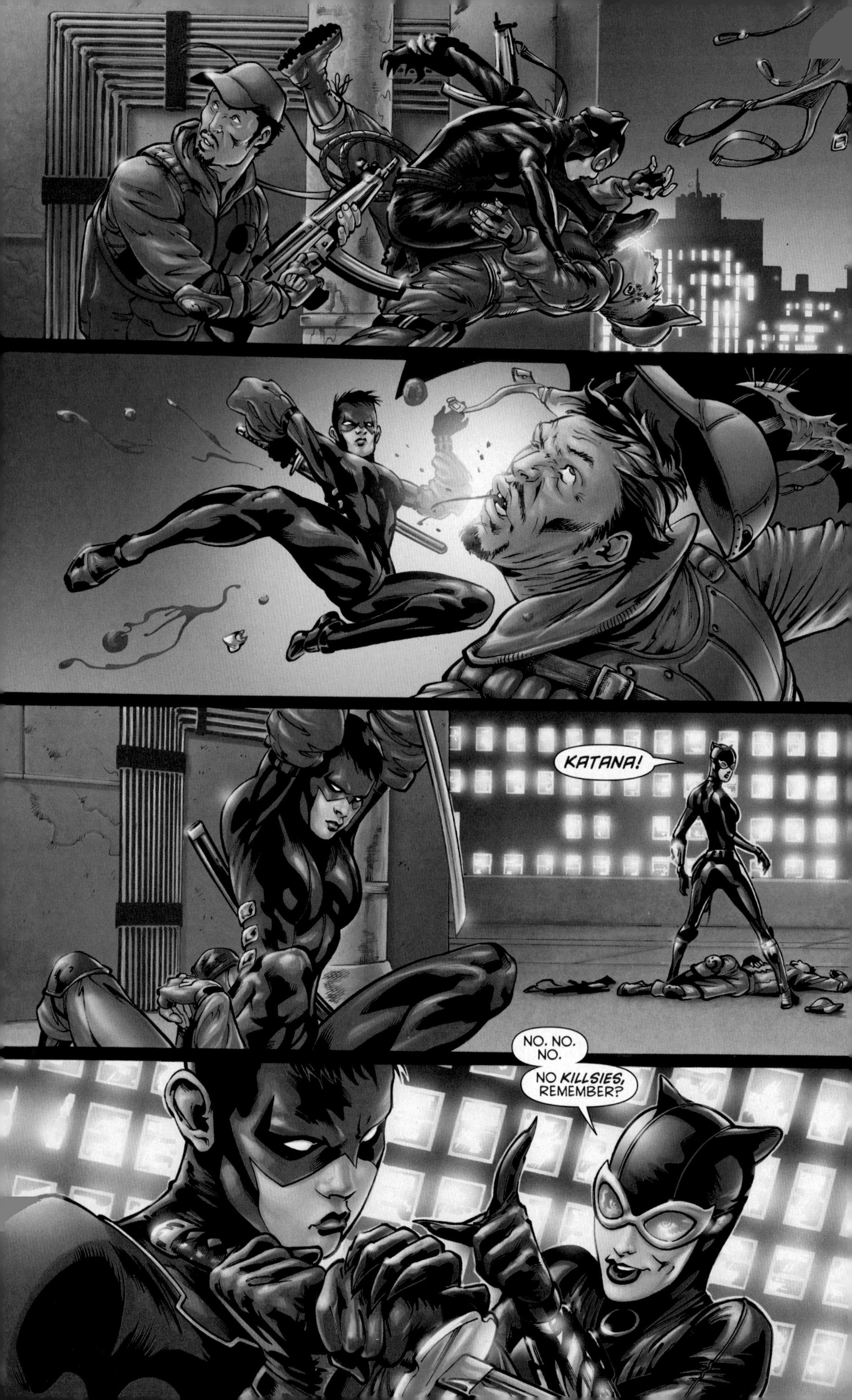
KATANA!
NO. NO. NO.
NO KILLSIES, REMEMBER?

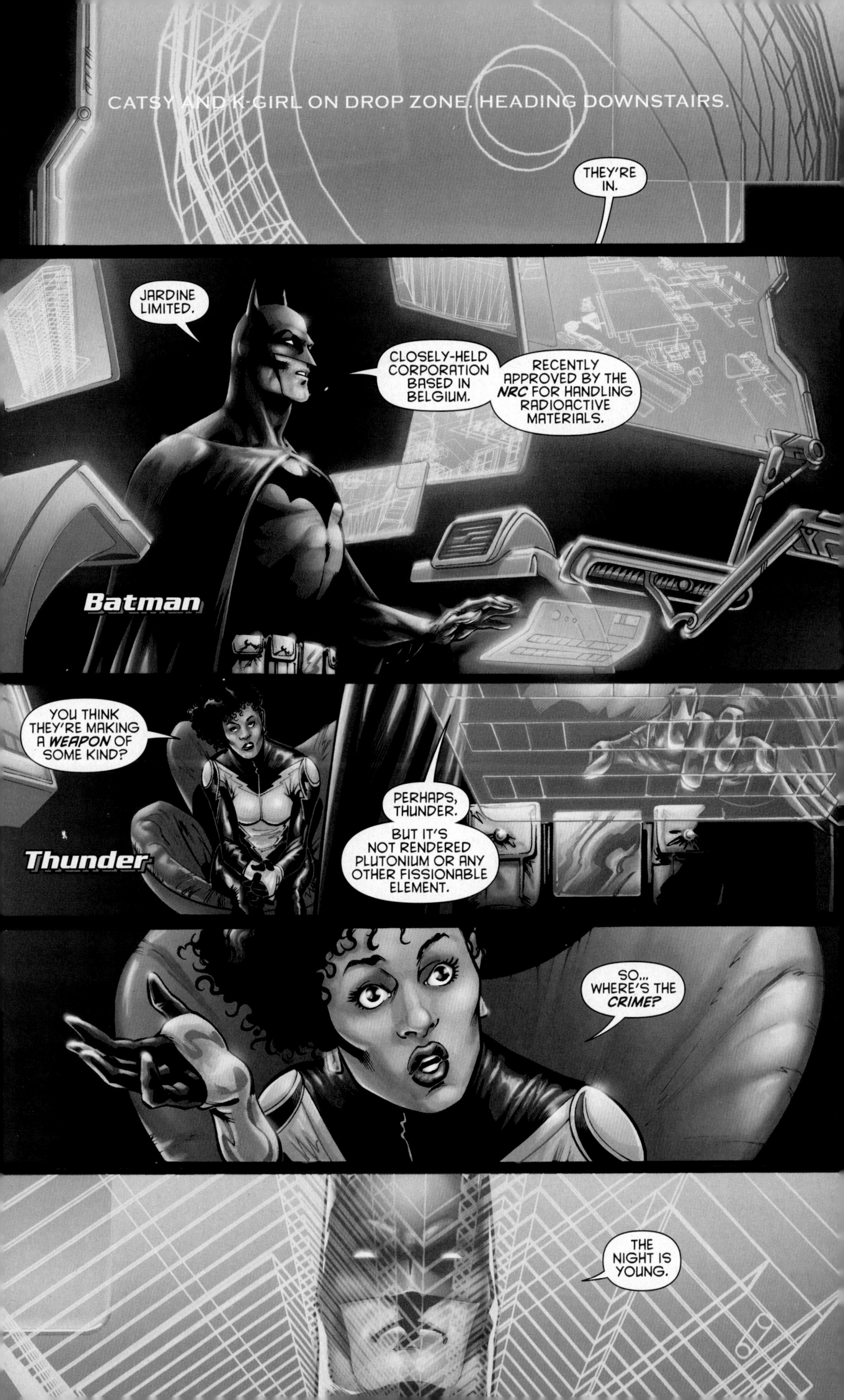
CATSY AND K-GIRL ON DROP ZONE. HEADING DOWNSTAIRS.
THEY'RE IN.
JARDINE LIMITED.
CLOSELY-HELD CORPORATION BASED IN BELGIUM.
RECENTLY APPROVED BY THE NRC FOR HANDLING RADIOACTIVE MATERIALS.
Batman
YOU THINK THEY'RE MAKING A WEAPON OF SOME KIND?
Thunder
PERHAPS, THUNDER.
BUT IT'S NOT RENDERED PLUTONIUM OR ANY OTHER FISSIONABLE ELEMENT.
SO... WHERE'S THE CRIME?
THE NIGHT IS YOUNG.

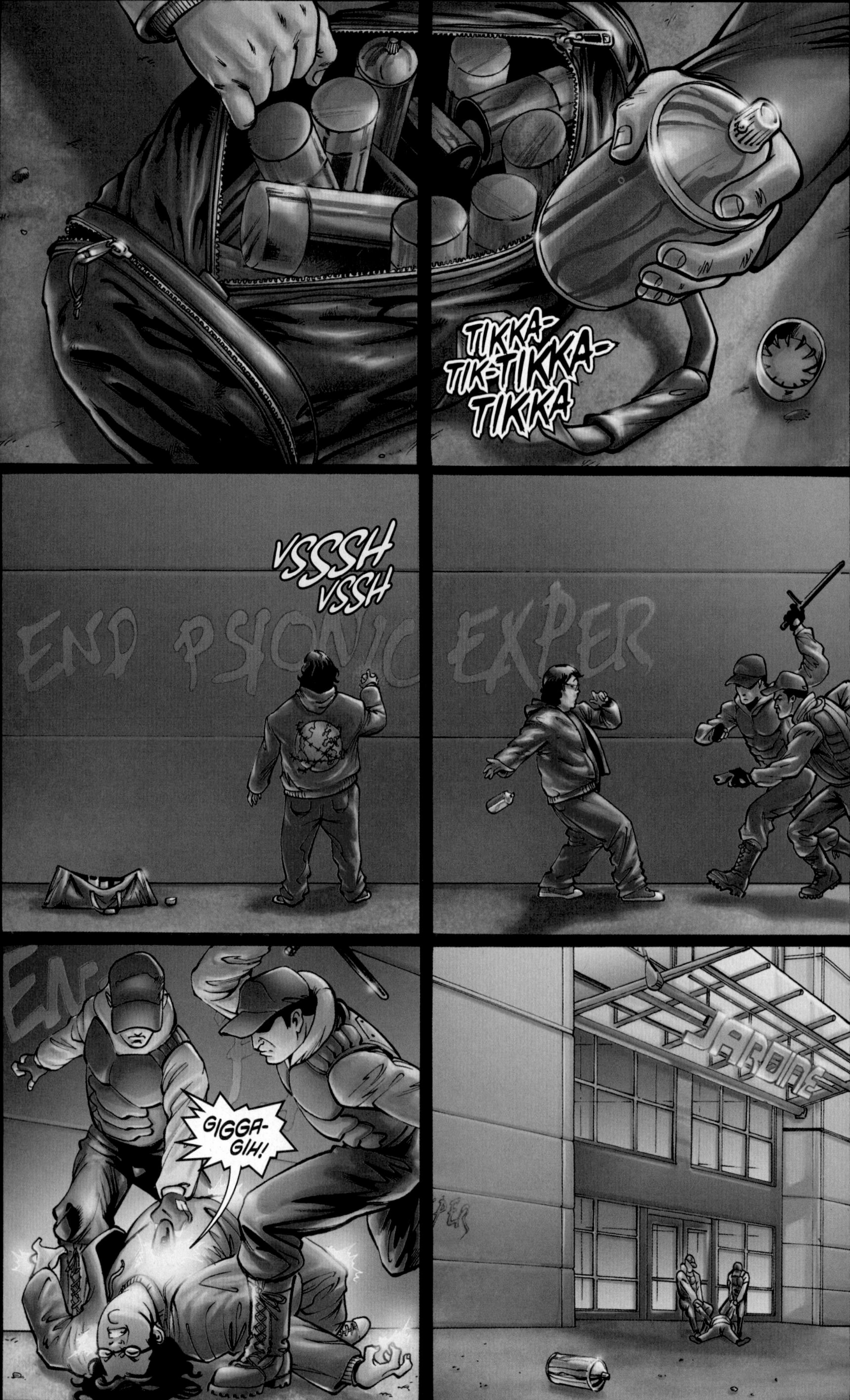
TIKKA-
TIK-TIKKA-
TIKKA
VSSSH
VSSH
END PSIONIC EXPER
GIGGA-
GIH!
JARDINE

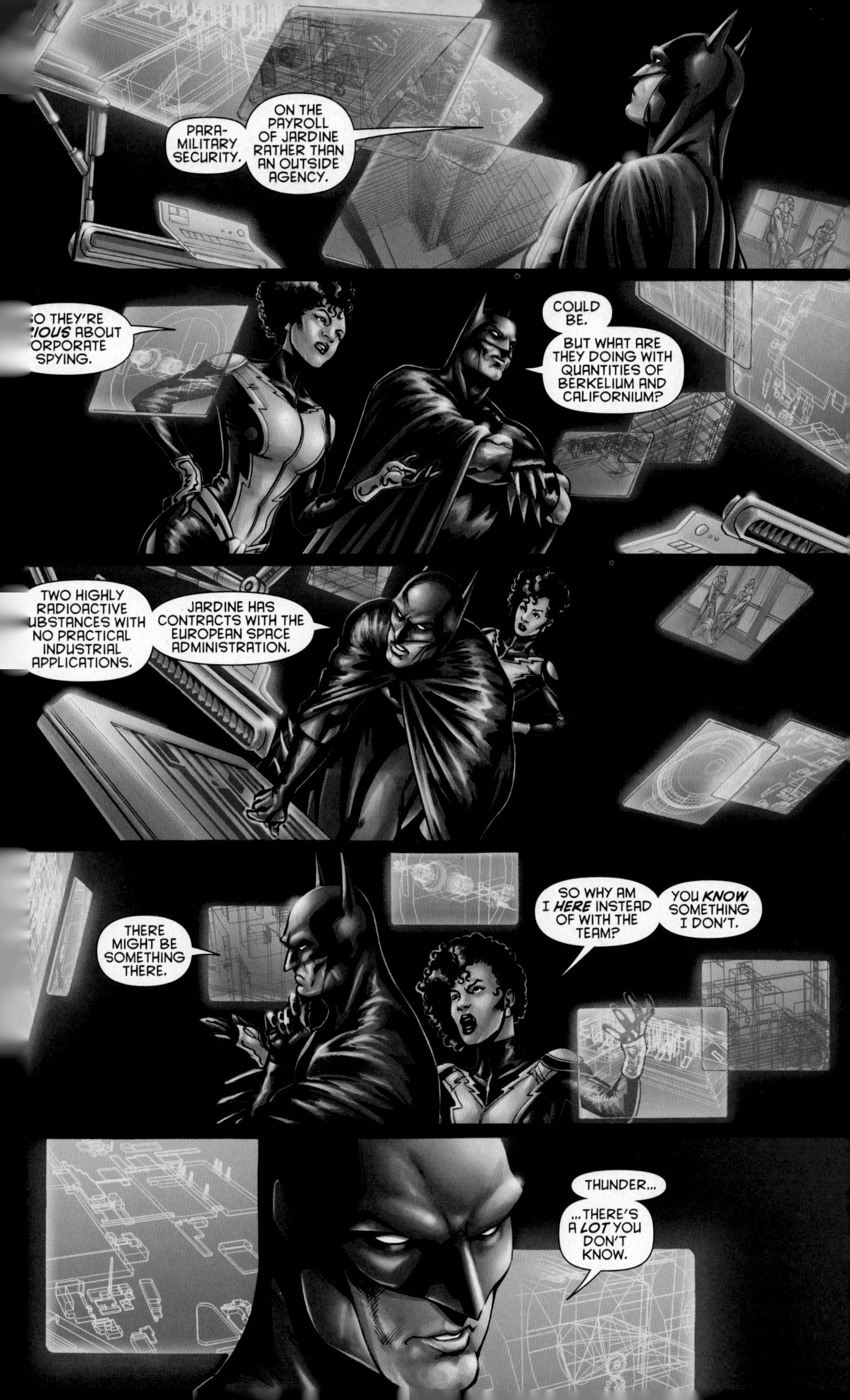
PARA-MILITARY SECURITY.
ON THE PAYROLL OF JARDINE RATHER THAN AN OUTSIDE AGENCY.
O THEY'RE RIOUS ABOUT ORPORATE SPYING.
COULD BE.
BUT WHAT ARE THEY DOING WITH QUANTITIES OF BERKELIUM AND CALIFORNIUM?
TWO HIGHLY RADIOACTIVE UBSTANCES WITH NO PRACTICAL INDUSTRIAL APPLICATIONS.
JARDINE HAS CONTRACTS WITH THE EUROPEAN SPACE ADMINISTRATION.
THERE MIGHT BE SOMETHING THERE.
SO WHY AM I HERE INSTEAD OF WITH THE TEAM?
YOU KNOW SOMETHING I DON'T.
THUNDER...
...THERE'S A LOT YOU DON'T KNOW.

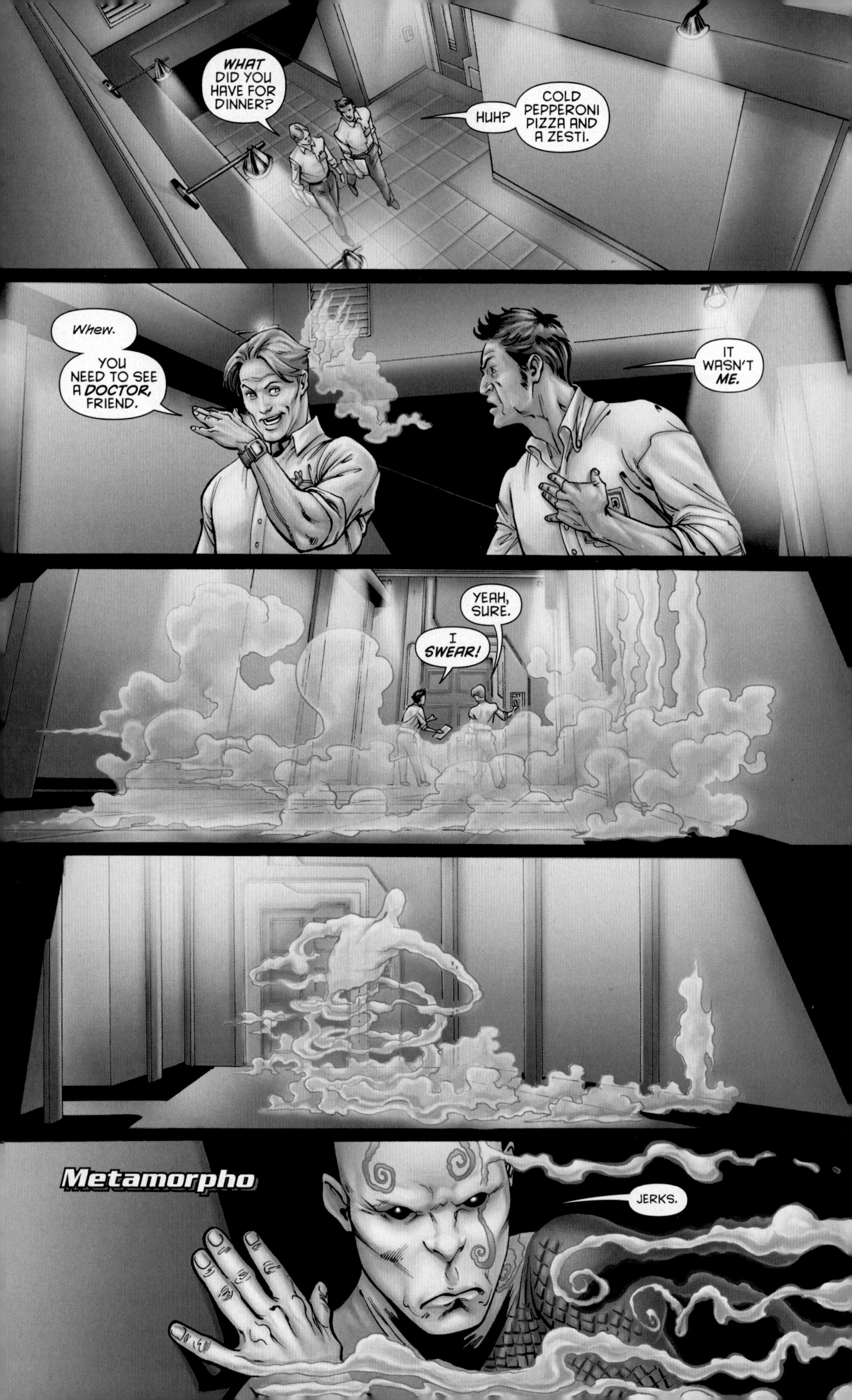
WHAT DID YOU HAVE FOR DINNER?
HUH?
COLD PEPPERONI PIZZA AND A ZESTI.
Whew.
YOU NEED TO SEE A DOCTOR, FRIEND.
IT WASN'T ME.
YEAH, SURE.
I SWEAR!
Metamorpho
JERKS.

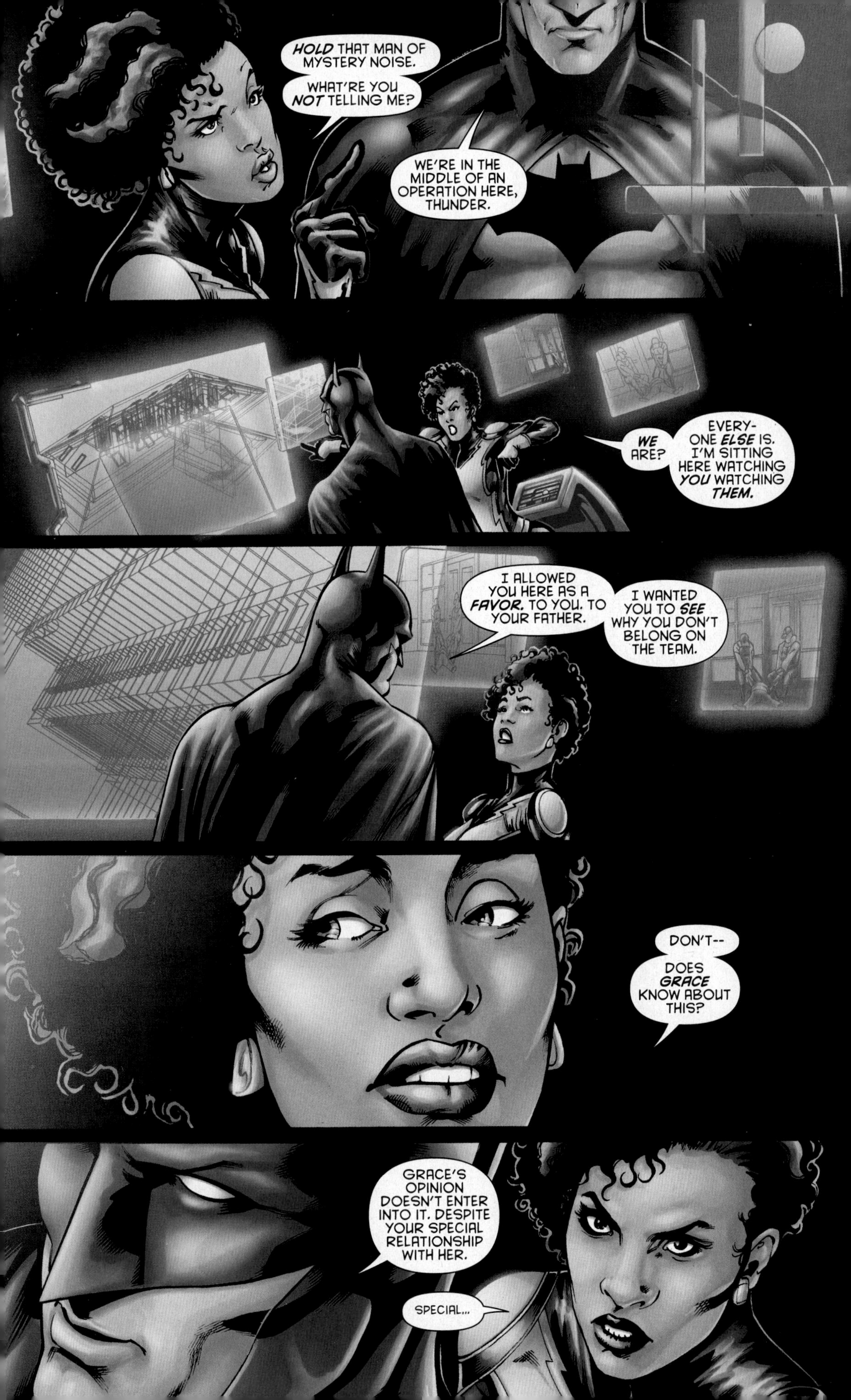
HOLD THAT MAN OF MYSTERY NOISE.
WHAT'RE YOU NOT TELLING ME?
WE'RE IN THE MIDDLE OF AN OPERATION HERE, THUNDER.
WE ARE?
EVERY-ONE ELSE IS. I'M SITTING HERE WATCHING YOU WATCHING THEM.
I ALLOWED YOU HERE AS A FAVOR. TO YOU. TO YOUR FATHER.
I WANTED YOU TO SEE WHY YOU DON'T BELONG ON THE TEAM.
DON'T--
DOES GRACE KNOW ABOUT THIS?
GRACE'S OPINION DOESN'T ENTER INTO IT. DESPITE YOUR SPECIAL RELATIONSHIP WITH HER.
SPECIAL...

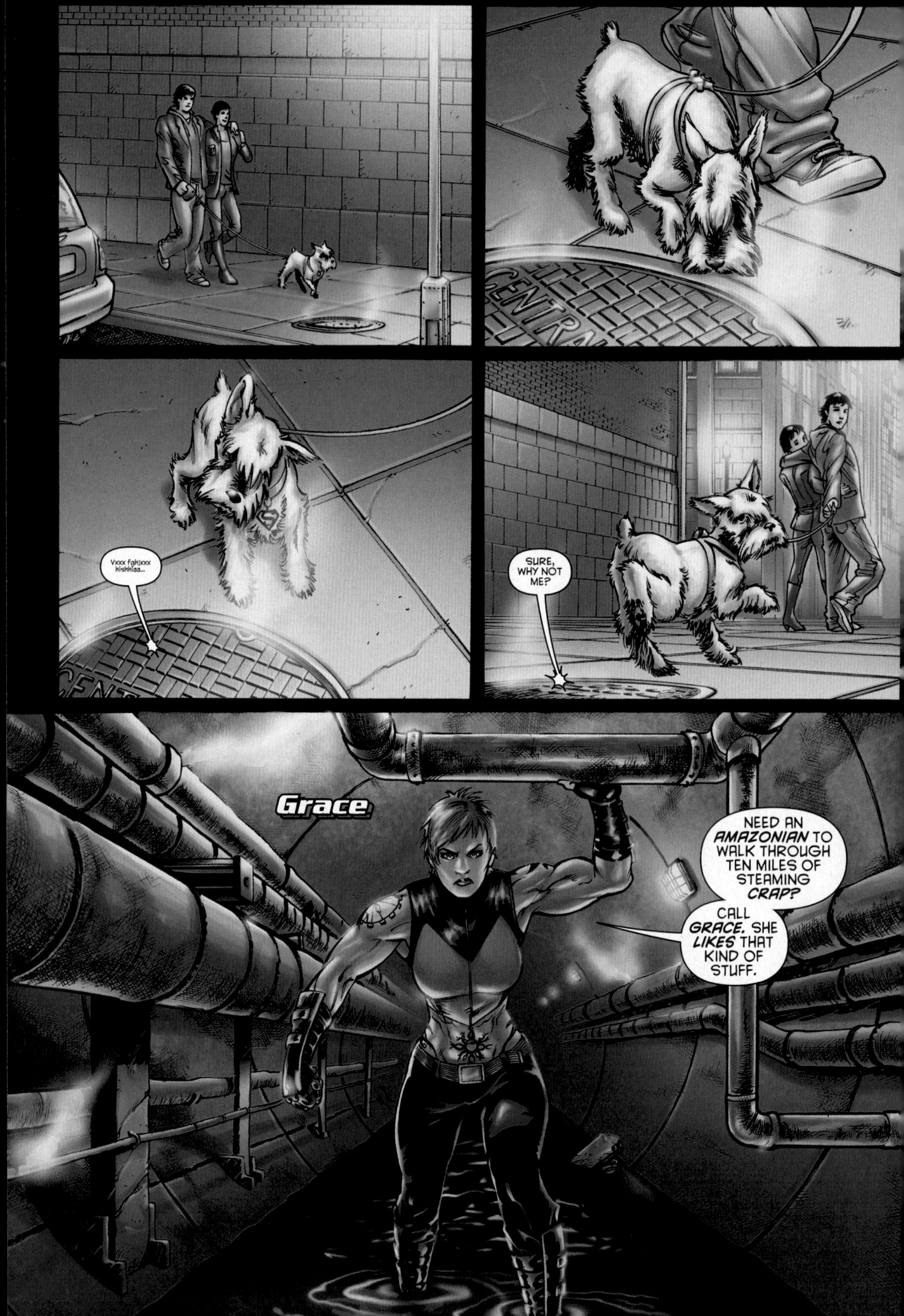
Vxxx fghjxxx hishhiaa...
SURE, WHY NOT ME?
Grace
NEED AN AMAZONIAN TO WALK THROUGH TEN MILES OF STEAMING CRAP?
CALL GRACE. SHE LIKES THAT KIND OF STUFF.

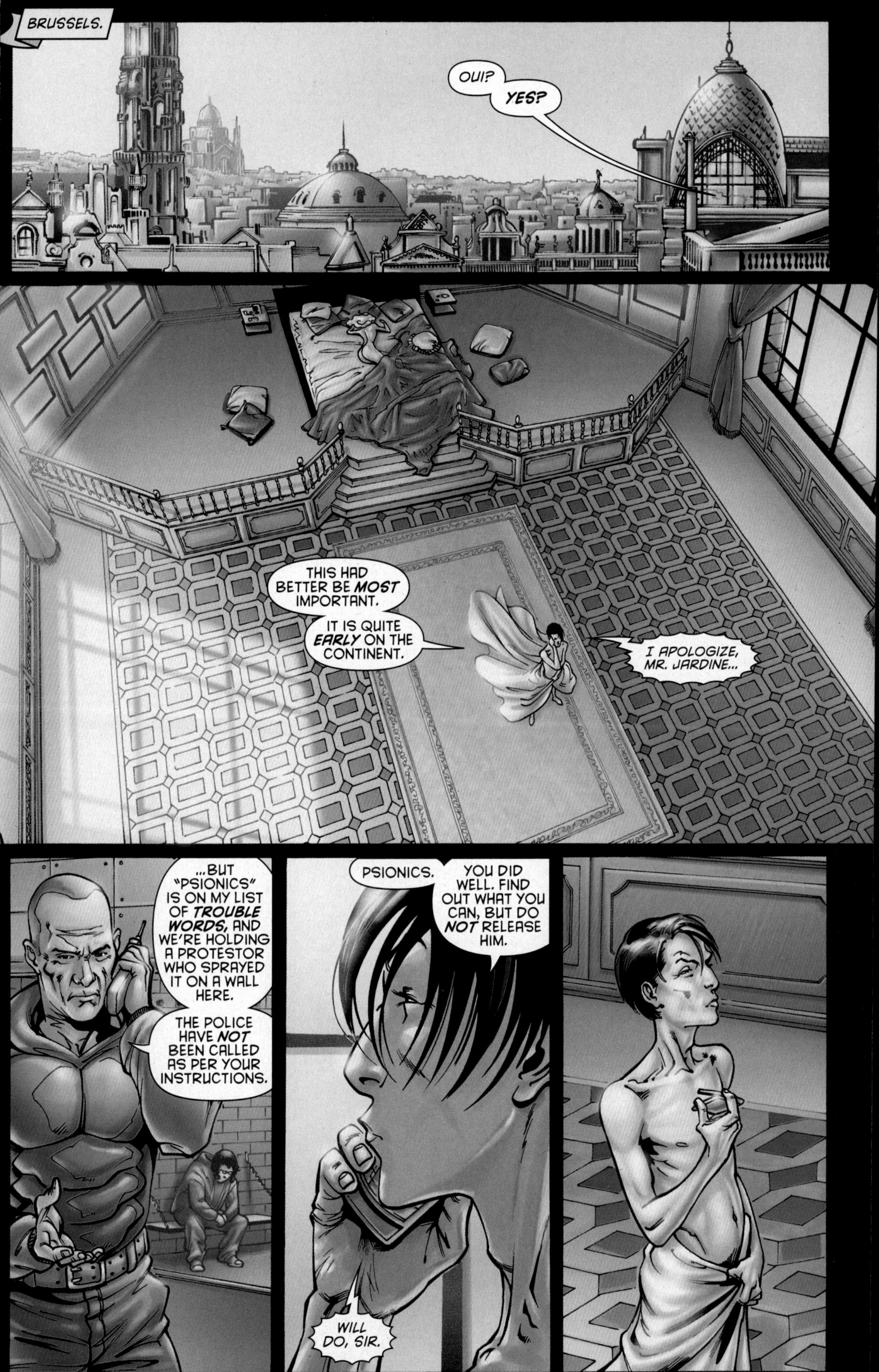
BRUSSELS.
OUI?
YES?
THIS HAD BETTER BE MOST IMPORTANT.
IT IS QUITE EARLY ON THE CONTINENT.
I APOLOGIZE, MR. JARDINE...
...BUT "PSIONICS" IS ON MY LIST OF TROUBLE WORDS, AND WE'RE HOLDING A PROTESTOR WHO SPRAYED IT ON A WALL HERE.
THE POLICE HAVE NOT BEEN CALLED AS PER YOUR INSTRUCTIONS.
PSIONICS.
YOU DID WELL. FIND OUT WHAT YOU CAN, BUT DO NOT RELEASE HIM.
WILL DO, SIR.

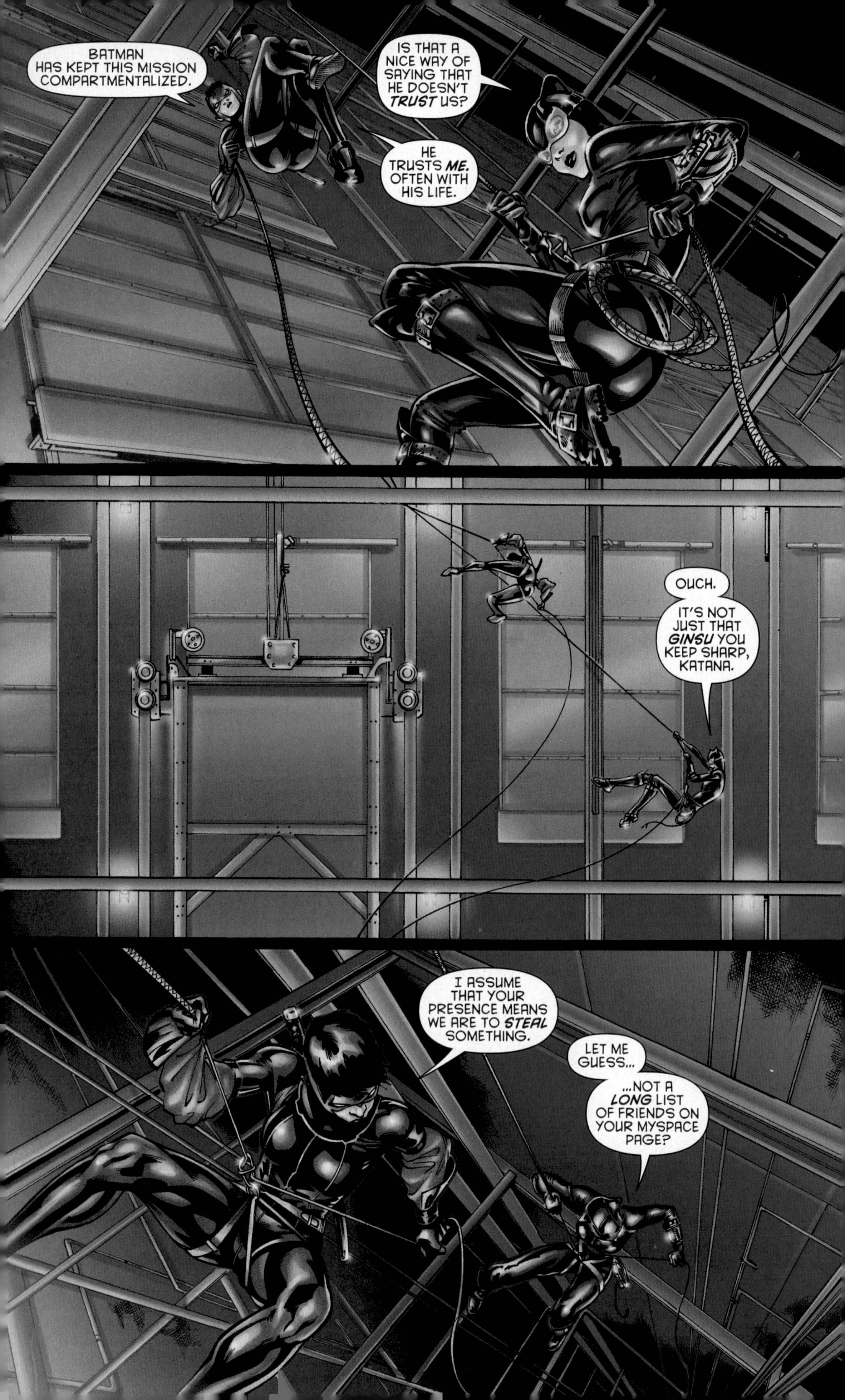
BATMAN HAS KEPT THIS MISSION COMPARTMENTALIZED.
IS THAT A NICE WAY OF SAYING THAT HE DOESN'T TRUST US?
HE TRUSTS ME. OFTEN WITH HIS LIFE.
OUCH.
IT'S NOT JUST THAT GINSU YOU KEEP SHARP, KATANA.
I ASSUME THAT YOUR PRESENCE MEANS WE ARE TO STEAL SOMETHING.
LET ME GUESS...
...NOT A LONG LIST OF FRIENDS ON YOUR MYSPACE PAGE?

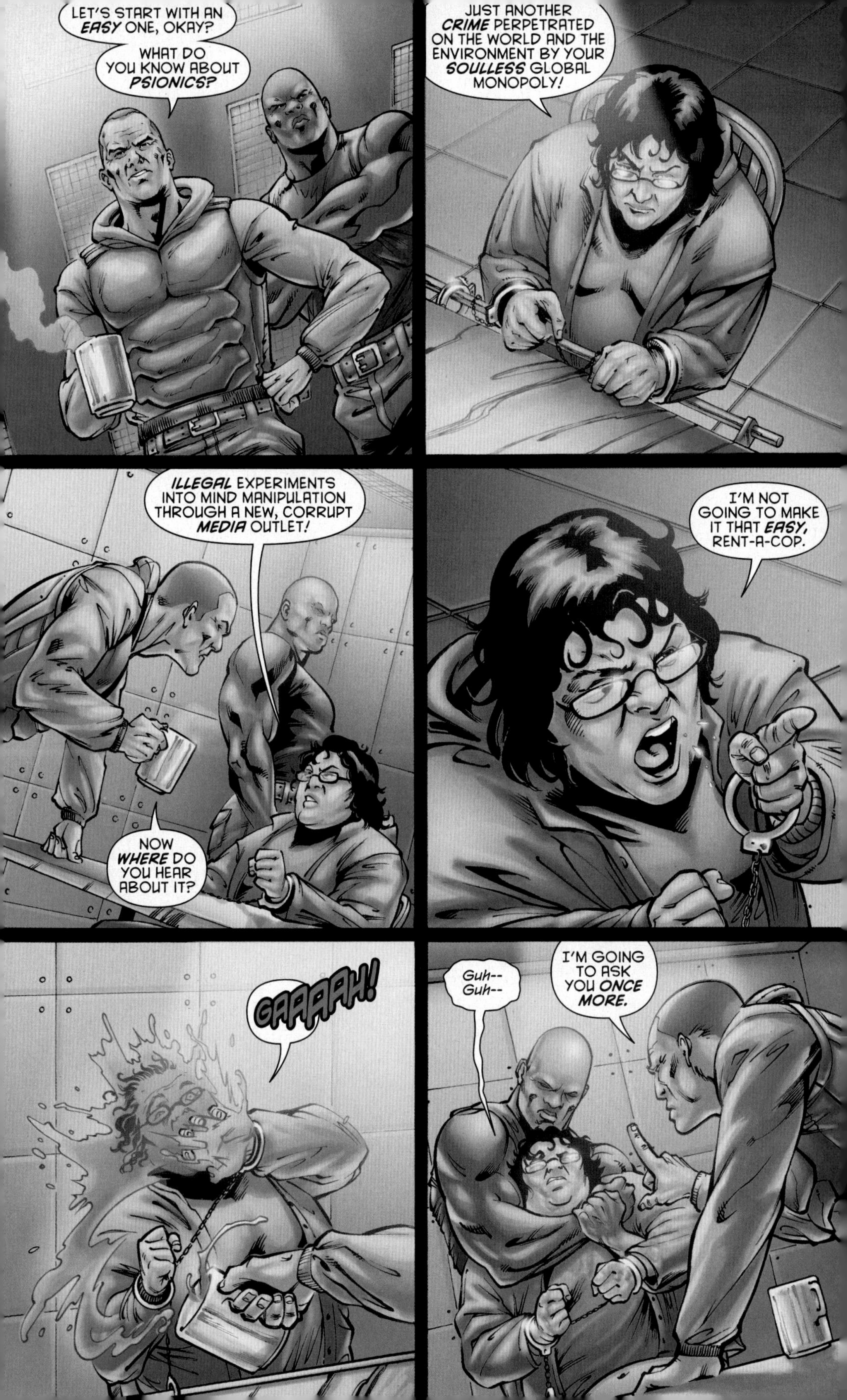
LET'S START WITH AN EASY ONE, OKAY?
WHAT DO YOU KNOW ABOUT PSIONICS?
JUST ANOTHER CRIME PERPETRATED ON THE WORLD AND THE ENVIRONMENT BY YOUR SOULLESS GLOBAL MONOPOLY!
ILLEGAL EXPERIMENTS INTO MIND MANIPULATION THROUGH A NEW, CORRUPT MEDIA OUTLET!
NOW WHERE DO YOU HEAR ABOUT IT?
I'M NOT GOING TO MAKE IT THAT EASY, RENT-A-COP.
GAAAAH!
Guh-- Guh--
I'M GOING TO ASK YOU ONCE MORE.

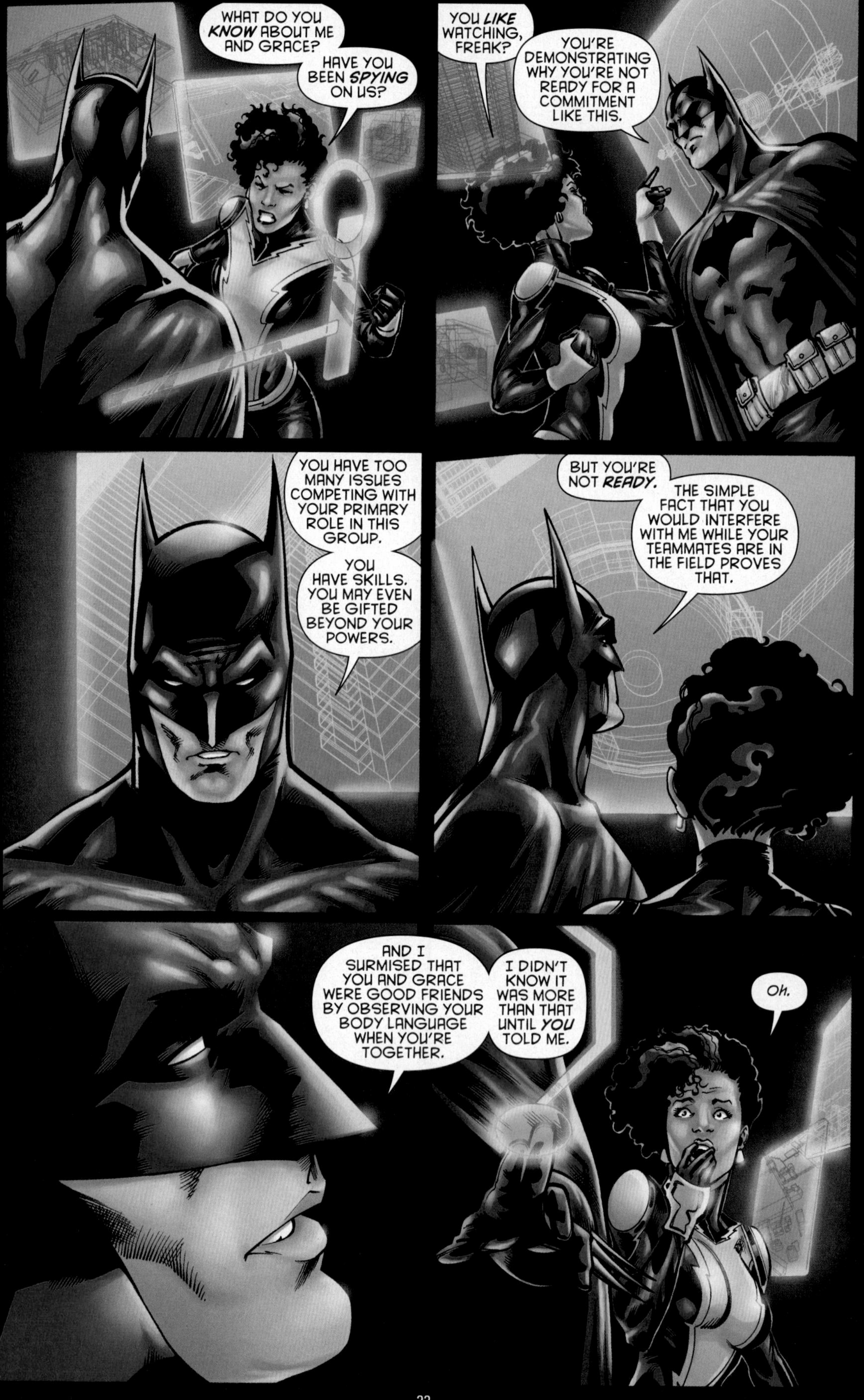
WHAT DO YOU KNOW ABOUT ME AND GRACE?
HAVE YOU BEEN SPYING ON US?
YOU LIKE WATCHING, FREAK?
YOU'RE DEMONSTRATING WHY YOU'RE NOT READY FOR A COMMITMENT LIKE THIS.
YOU HAVE TOO MANY ISSUES COMPETING WITH YOUR PRIMARY ROLE IN THIS GROUP.
YOU HAVE SKILLS. YOU MAY EVEN BE GIFTED BEYOND YOUR POWERS.
BUT YOU'RE NOT READY.
THE SIMPLE FACT THAT YOU WOULD INTERFERE WITH ME WHILE YOUR TEAMMATES ARE IN THE FIELD PROVES THAT.
AND I SURMISED THAT YOU AND GRACE WERE GOOD FRIENDS BY OBSERVING YOUR BODY LANGUAGE WHEN YOU'RE TOGETHER.
I DIDN'T KNOW IT WAS MORE THAN THAT UNTIL YOU TOLD ME.
Oh.

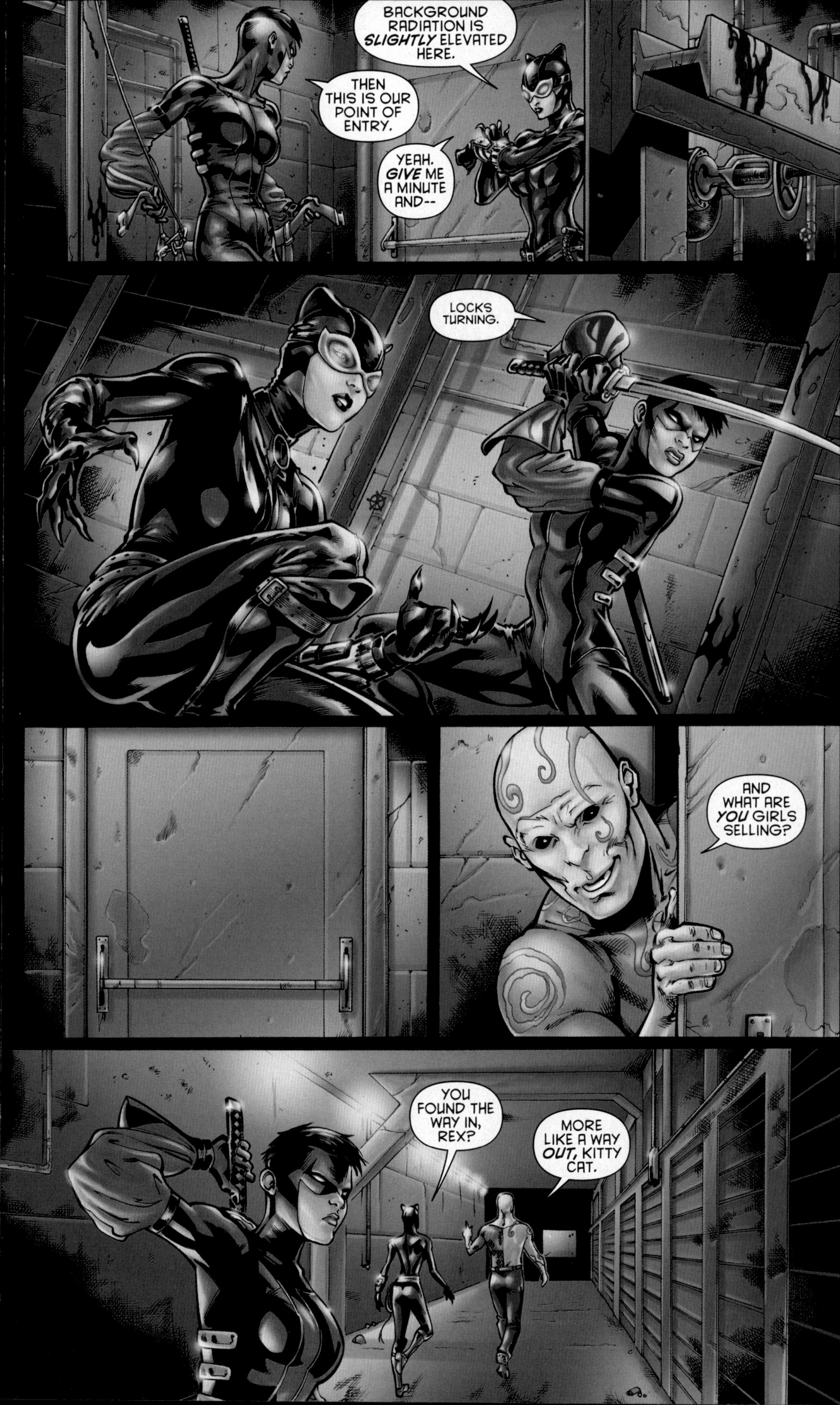
BACKGROUND RADIATION IS SLIGHTLY ELEVATED HERE.
THEN THIS IS OUR POINT OF ENTRY.
YEAH. GIVE ME A MINUTE AND--
LOCKS TURNING.
AND WHAT ARE YOU GIRLS SELLING?
YOU FOUND THE WAY IN, REX?
MORE LIKE A WAY OUT, KITTY CAT.

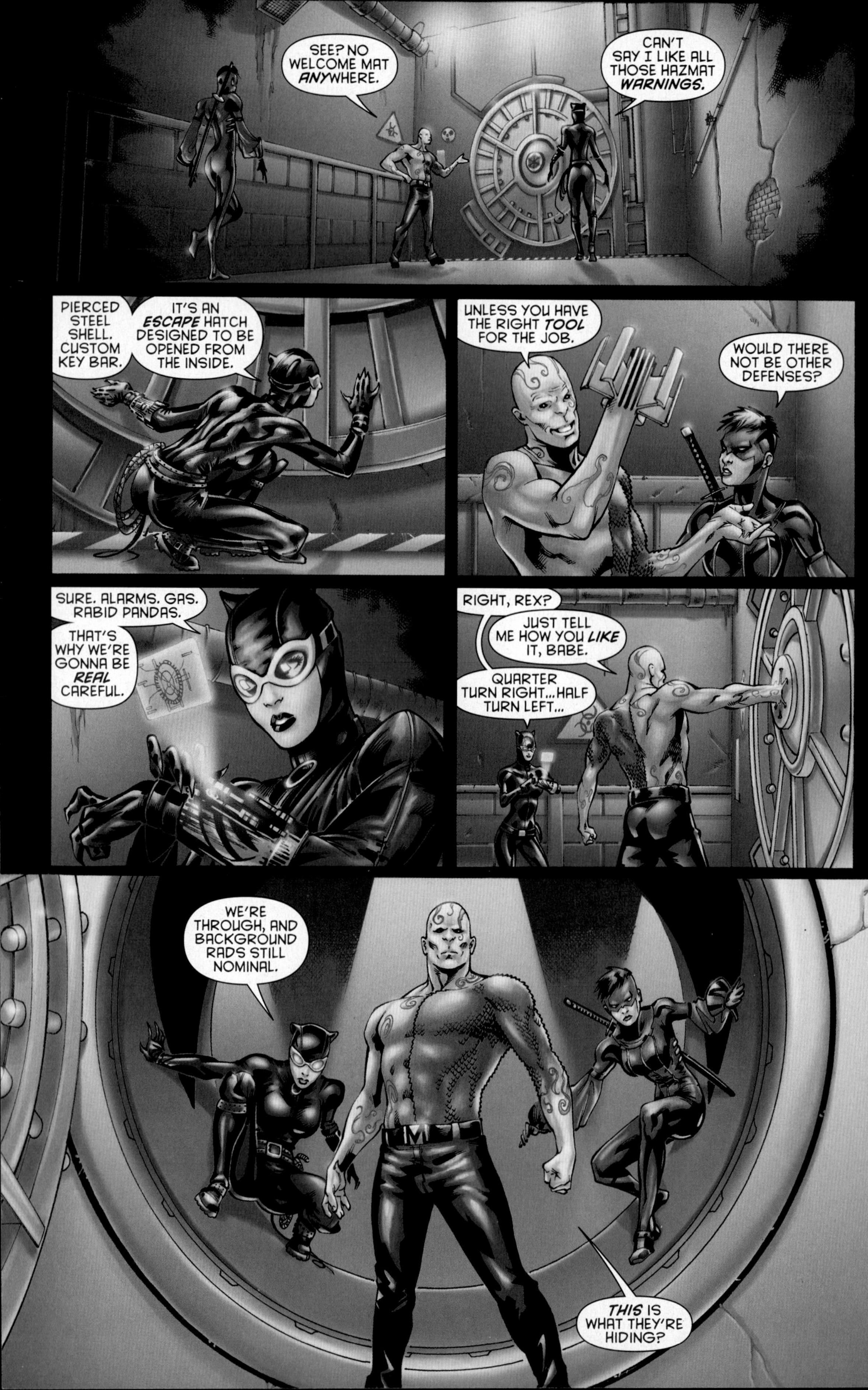
SEE? NO WELCOME MAT ANYWHERE.
CAN'T SAY I LIKE ALL THOSE HAZMAT WARNINGS.
PIERCED STEEL SHELL. CUSTOM KEY BAR.
IT'S AN ESCAPE HATCH DESIGNED TO BE OPENED FROM THE INSIDE.
UNLESS YOU HAVE THE RIGHT TOOL FOR THE JOB.
WOULD THERE NOT BE OTHER DEFENSES?
SURE. ALARMS. GAS. RABID PANDAS.
THAT'S WHY WE'RE GONNA BE REAL CAREFUL.
RIGHT, REX?
JUST TELL ME HOW YOU LIKE IT, BABE.
QUARTER TURN RIGHT... HALF TURN LEFT...
WE'RE THROUGH, AND BACKGROUND RADS STILL NOMINAL.
THIS IS WHAT THEY'RE HIDING?

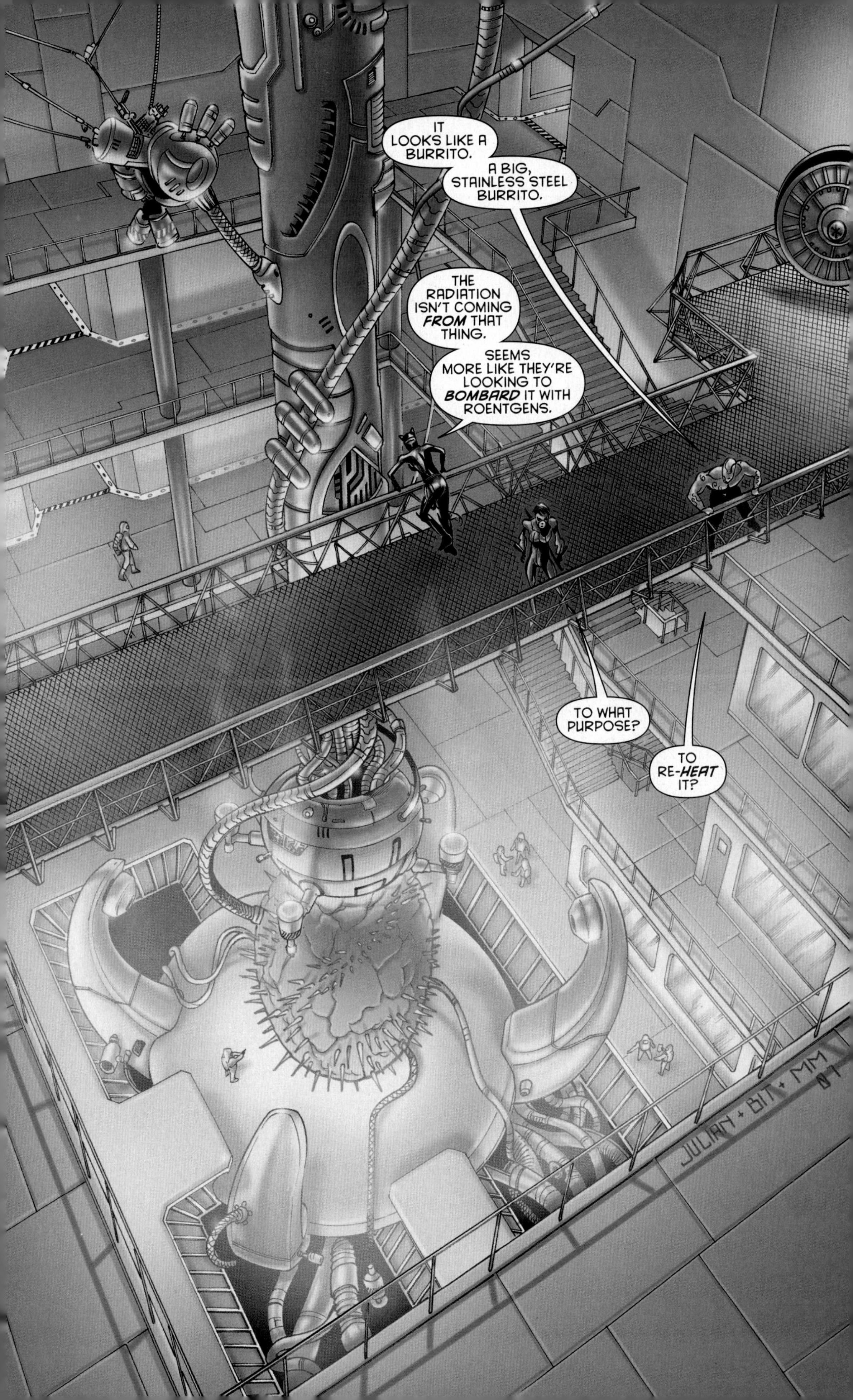
IT LOOKS LIKE A BURRITO.
A BIG, STAINLESS STEEL BURRITO.
THE RADIATION ISN'T COMING FROM THAT THING.
SEEMS MORE LIKE THEY'RE LOOKING TO BOMBARD IT WITH ROENTGENS.
TO WHAT PURPOSE?
TO RE-HEAT IT?
JULIAN + BIT + MM 01

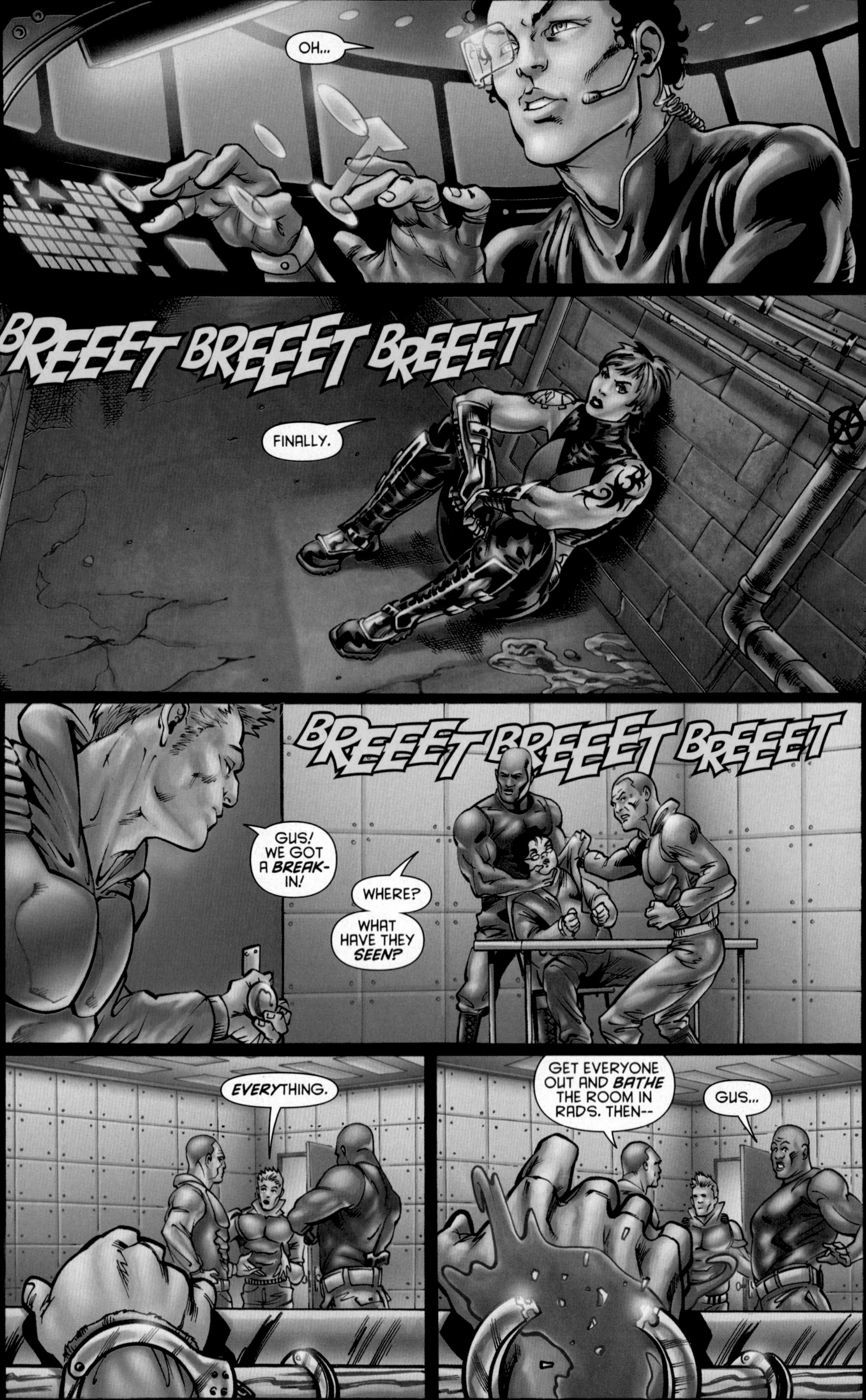
OH...
BREEET BREEET BREEET
FINALLY.
BREEET BREEET BREEET
GUS! WE GOT A BREAK-IN!
WHERE?
WHAT HAVE THEY SEEN?
EVERYTHING.
GET EVERYONE OUT AND BATHE THE ROOM IN RADS. THEN--
GUS...

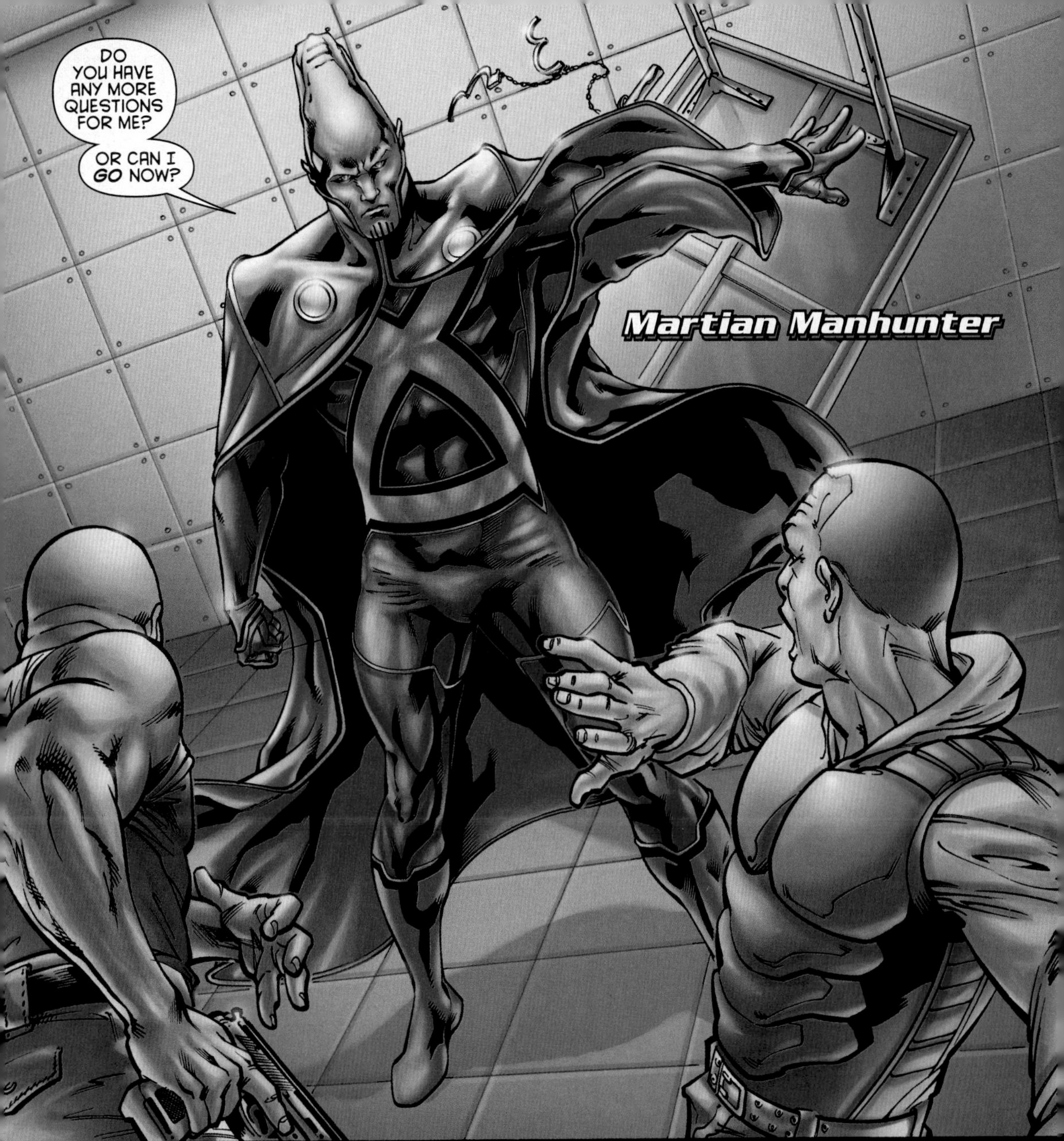
DO YOU HAVE ANY MORE QUESTIONS FOR ME?
OR CAN I GO NOW?
Martian Manhunter
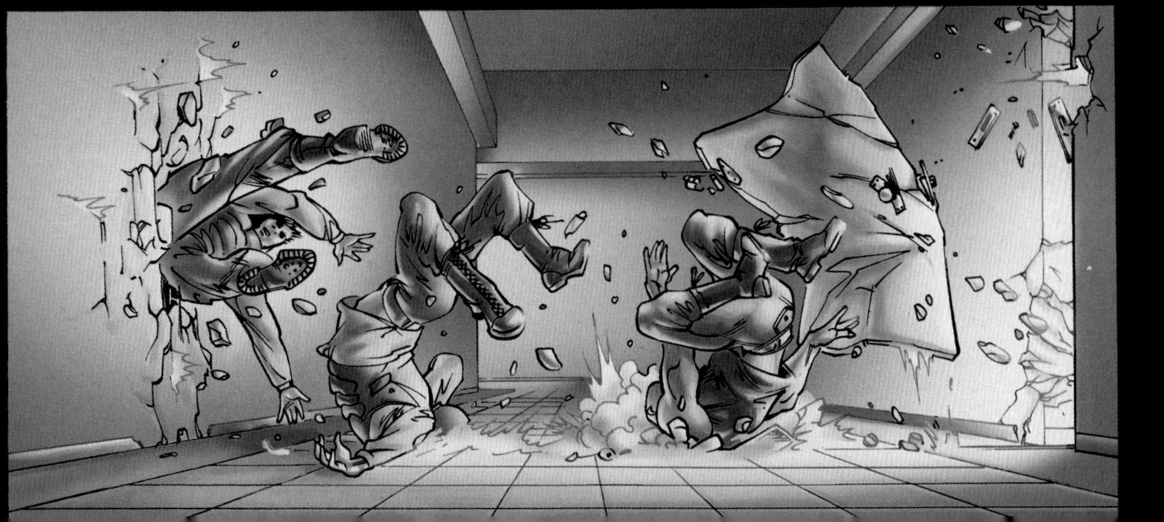

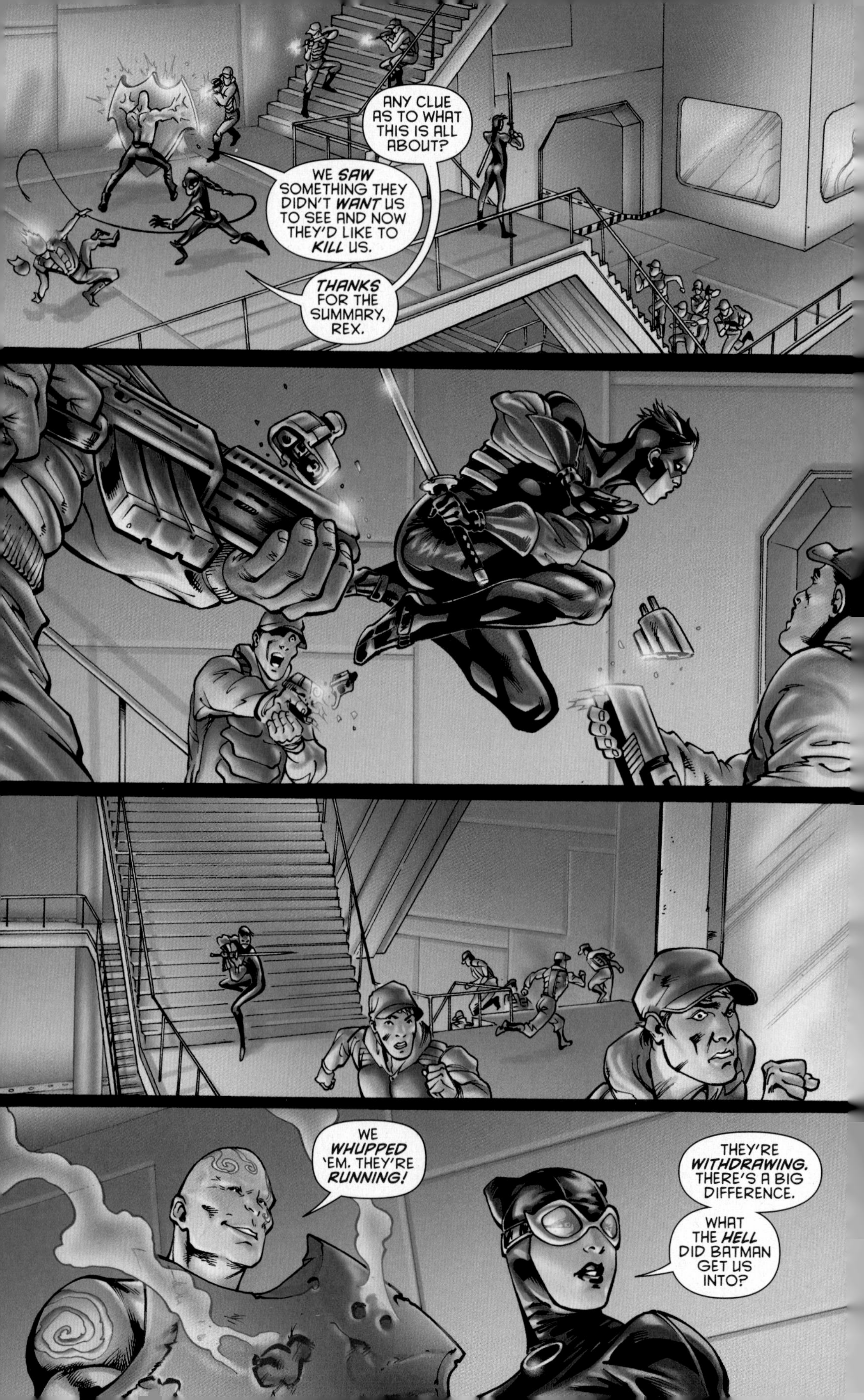
ANY CLUE AS TO WHAT THIS IS ALL ABOUT?
WE SAW SOMETHING THEY DIDN'T WANT US TO SEE AND NOW THEY'D LIKE TO KILL US.
THANKS FOR THE SUMMARY, REX.
WE WHUPPED 'EM. THEY'RE RUNNING!
THEY'RE WITHDRAWING. THERE'S A BIG DIFFERENCE.
WHAT THE HELL DID BATMAN GET US INTO?

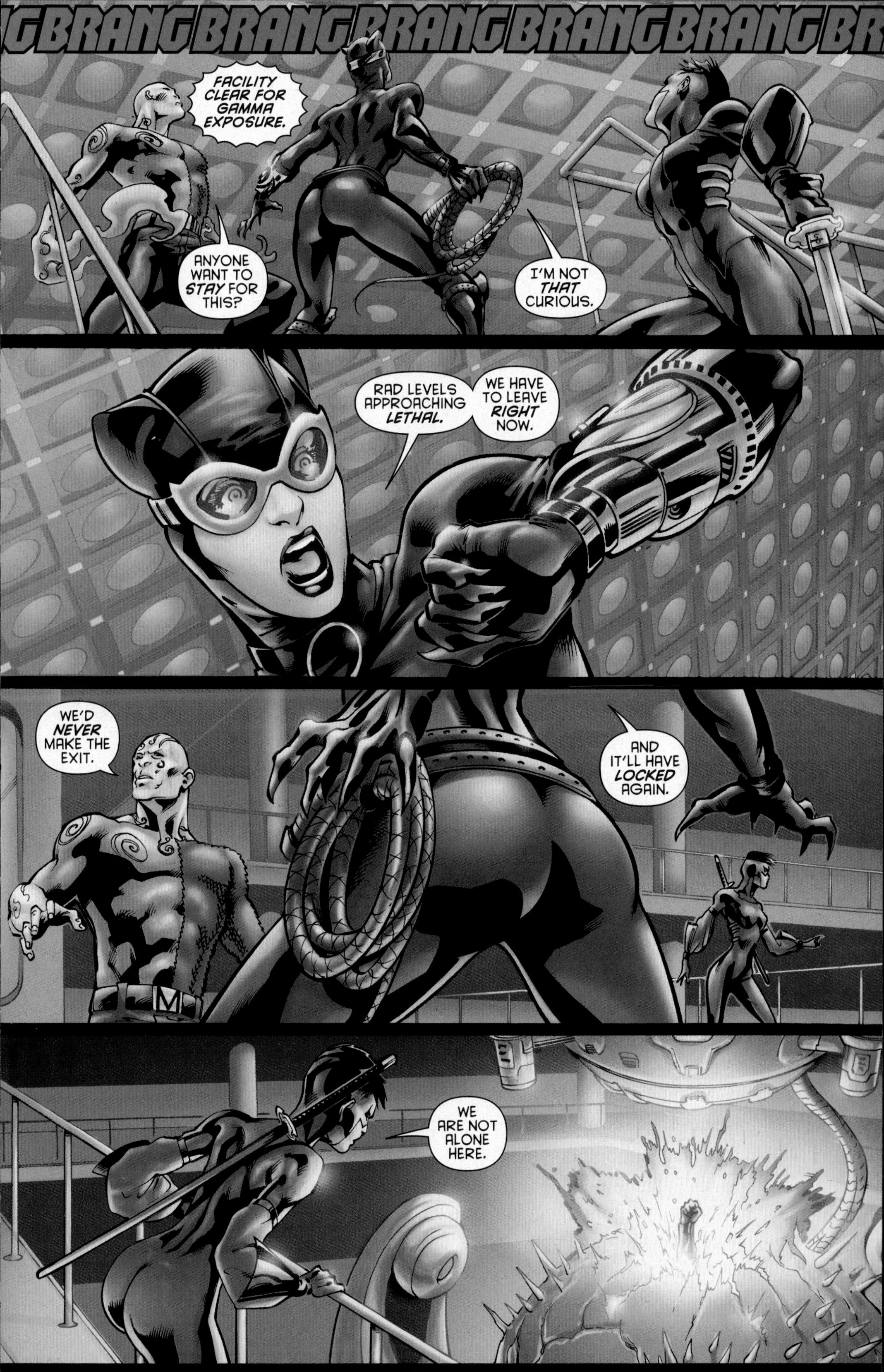
BRANG BRANG BRANG BRANG BRANG
FACILITY CLEAR FOR GAMMA EXPOSURE.
ANYONE WANT TO STAY FOR THIS?
I'M NOT THAT CURIOUS.
RAD LEVELS APPROACHING LETHAL.
WE HAVE TO LEAVE RIGHT NOW.
WE'D NEVER MAKE THE EXIT.
AND IT'LL HAVE LOCKED AGAIN.
WE ARE NOT ALONE HERE.

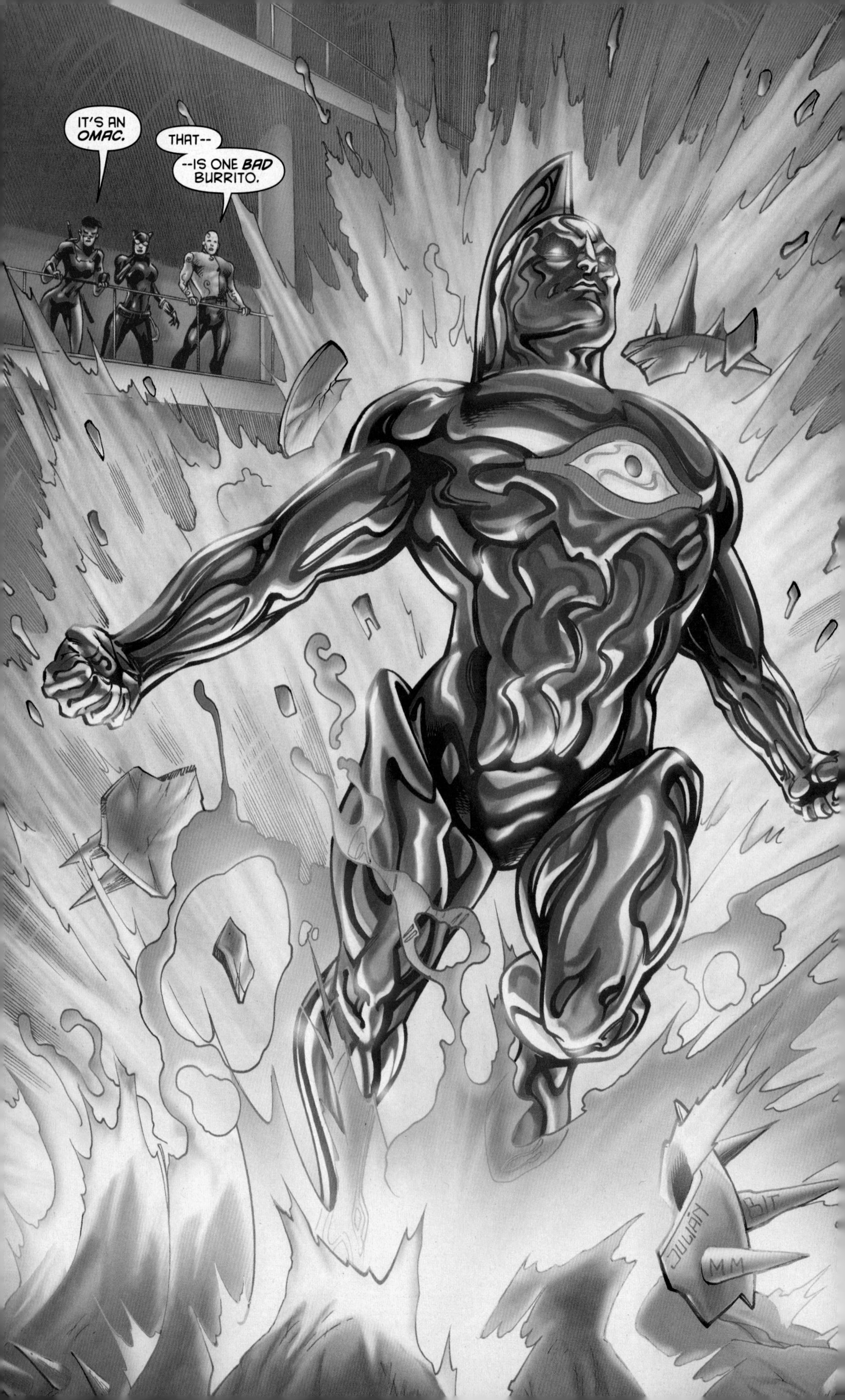
IT'S AN OMAC.
THAT--
--IS ONE BAD BURRITO.

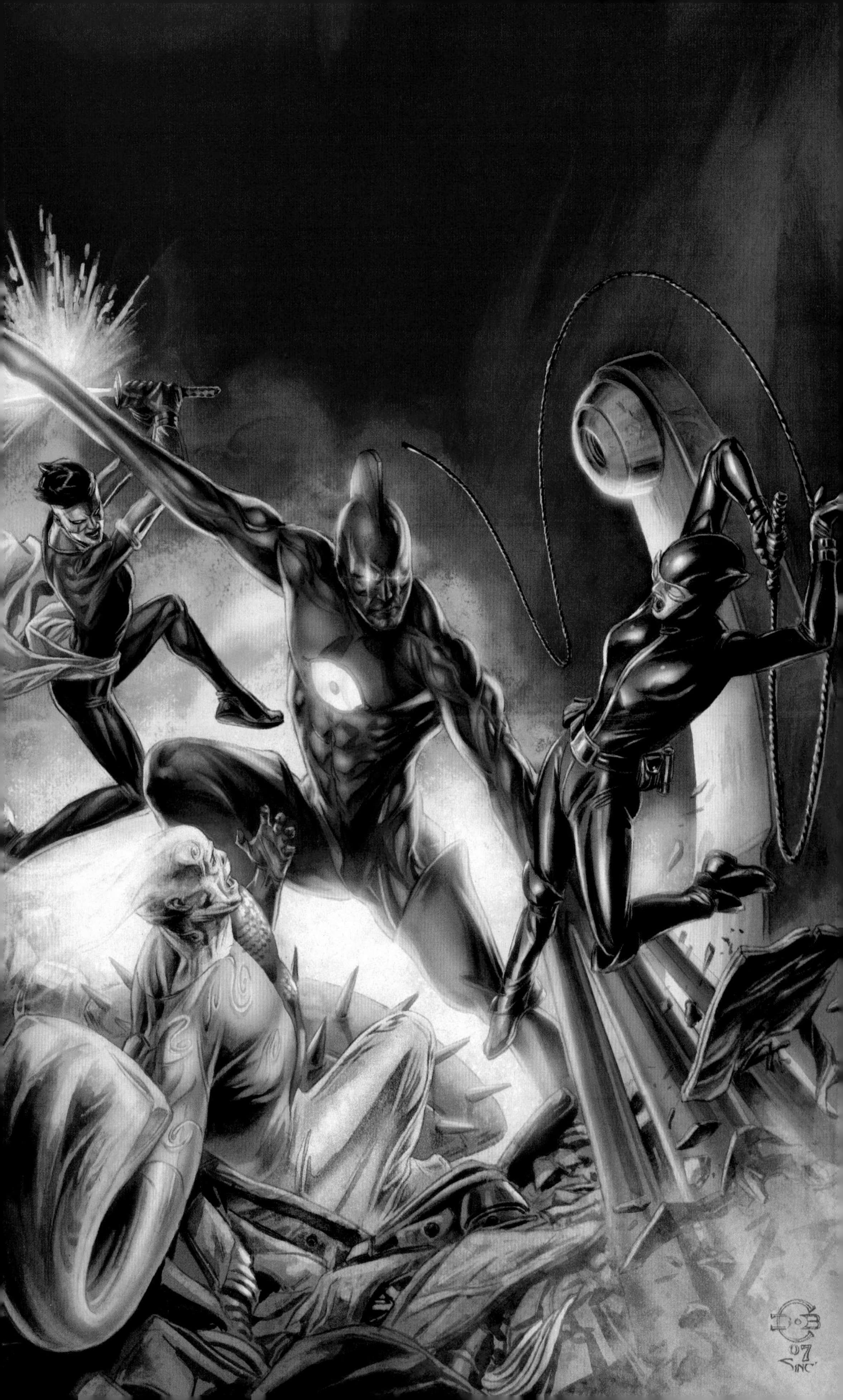

part TWO

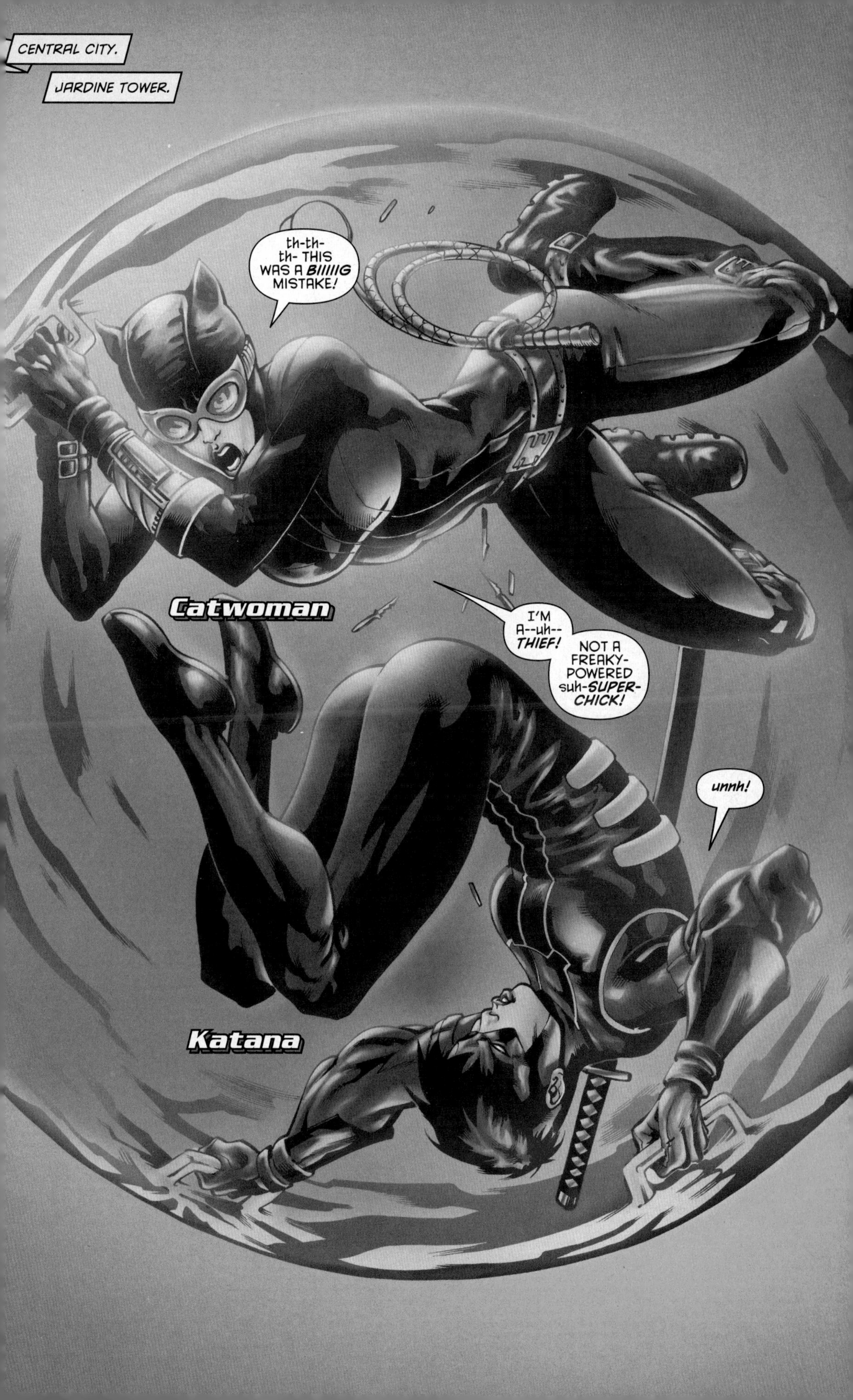
CENTRAL CITY.
JARDINE TOWER.
th-th- th- THIS WAS A BIIIIIG MISTAKE!
Catwoman
I'M A--uh-- THIEF!
NOT A FREAKY-POWERED suh-SUPER-CHICK!
unnh!
Katana

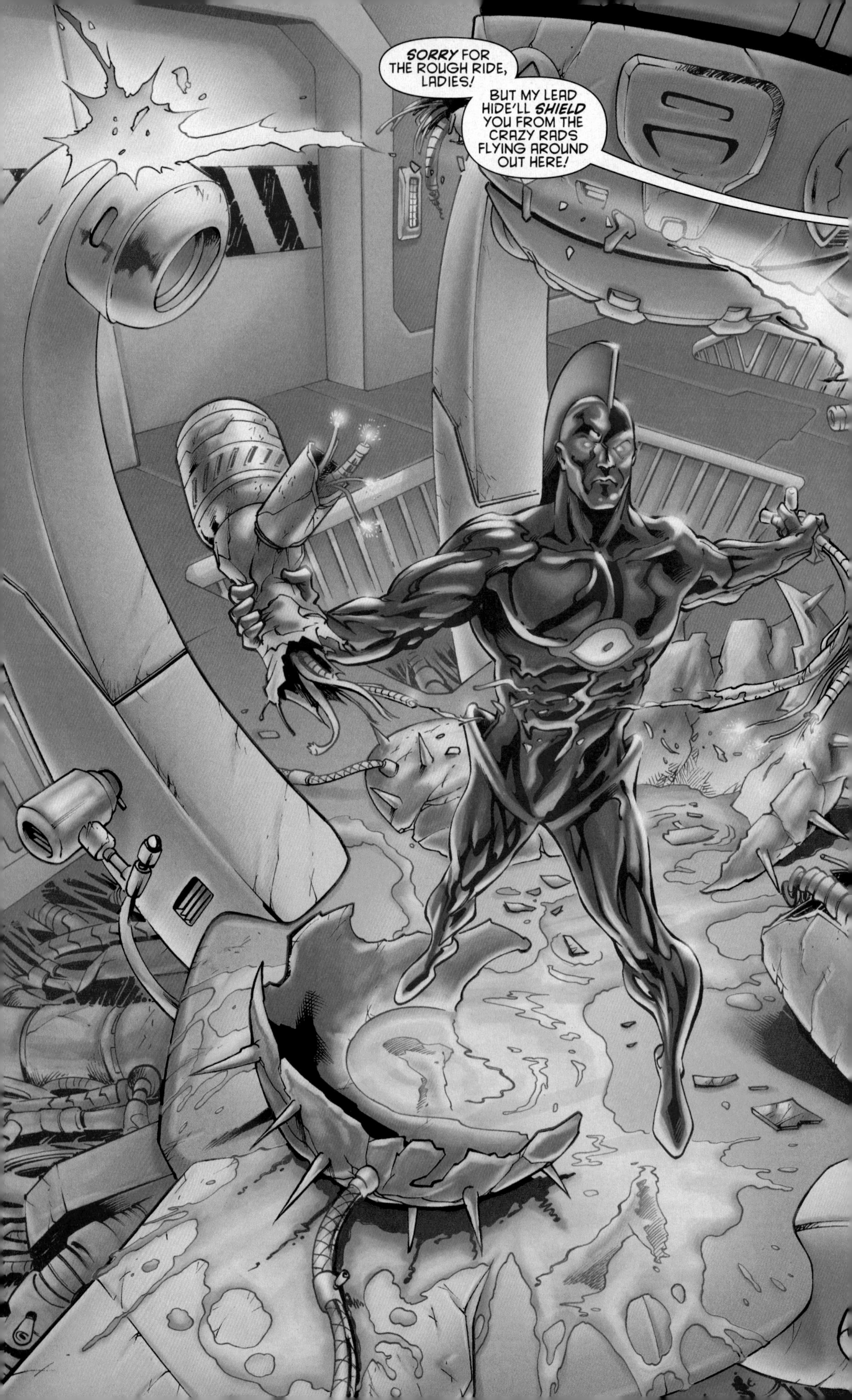
SORRY FOR THE ROUGH RIDE, LADIES!
BUT MY LEAD HIDE'LL SHIELD YOU FROM THE CRAZY RADS FLYING AROUND OUT HERE!

WE'RE GETTING AWAY FROM THIS OMAC RIGHT--
Metamorpho
INFESTATION

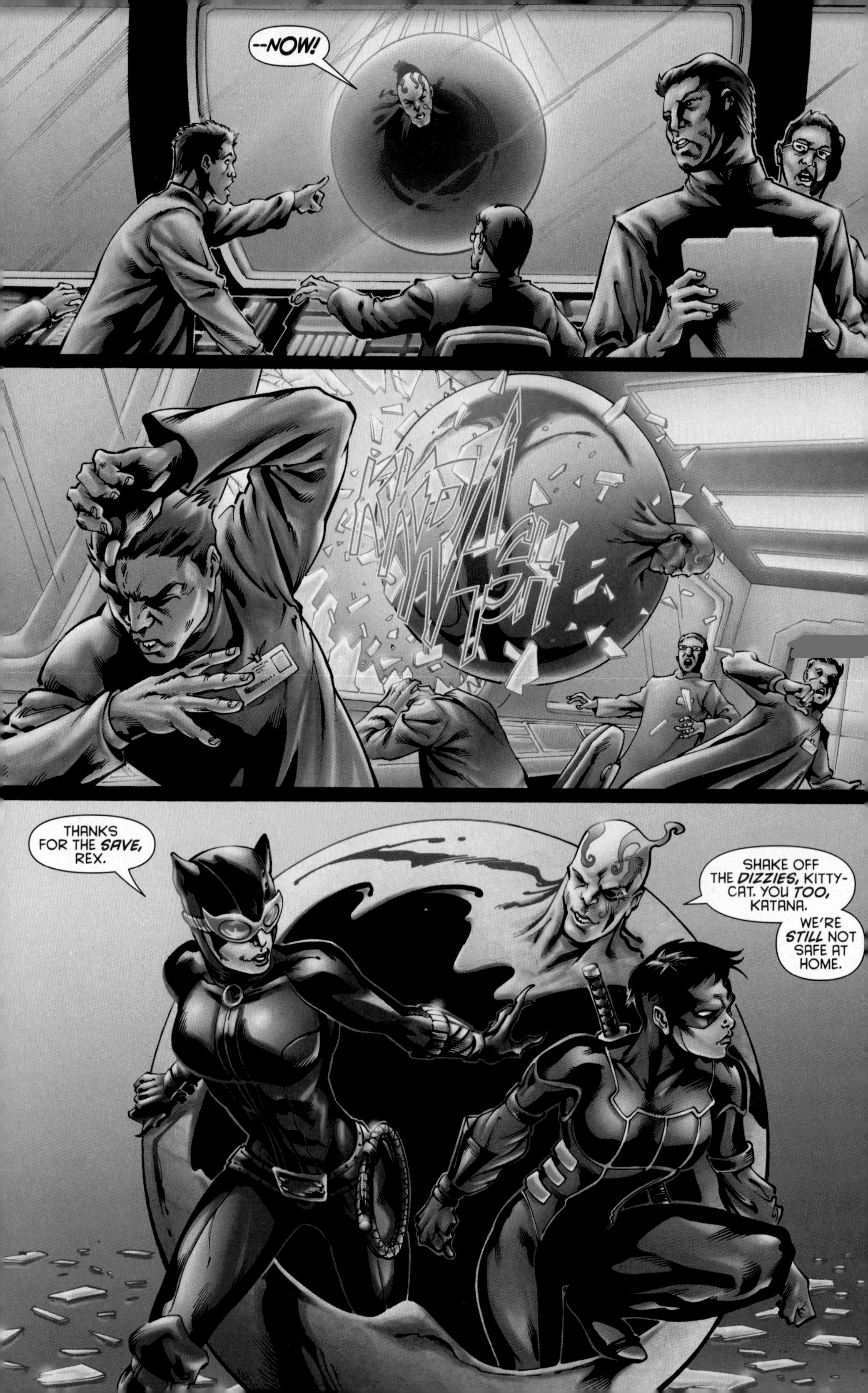
--NOW!
KKRRAASSH
THANKS FOR THE SAVE, REX.
SHAKE OFF THE DIZZIES, KITTY-CAT. YOU TOO, KATANA.
WE'RE STILL NOT SAFE AT HOME.

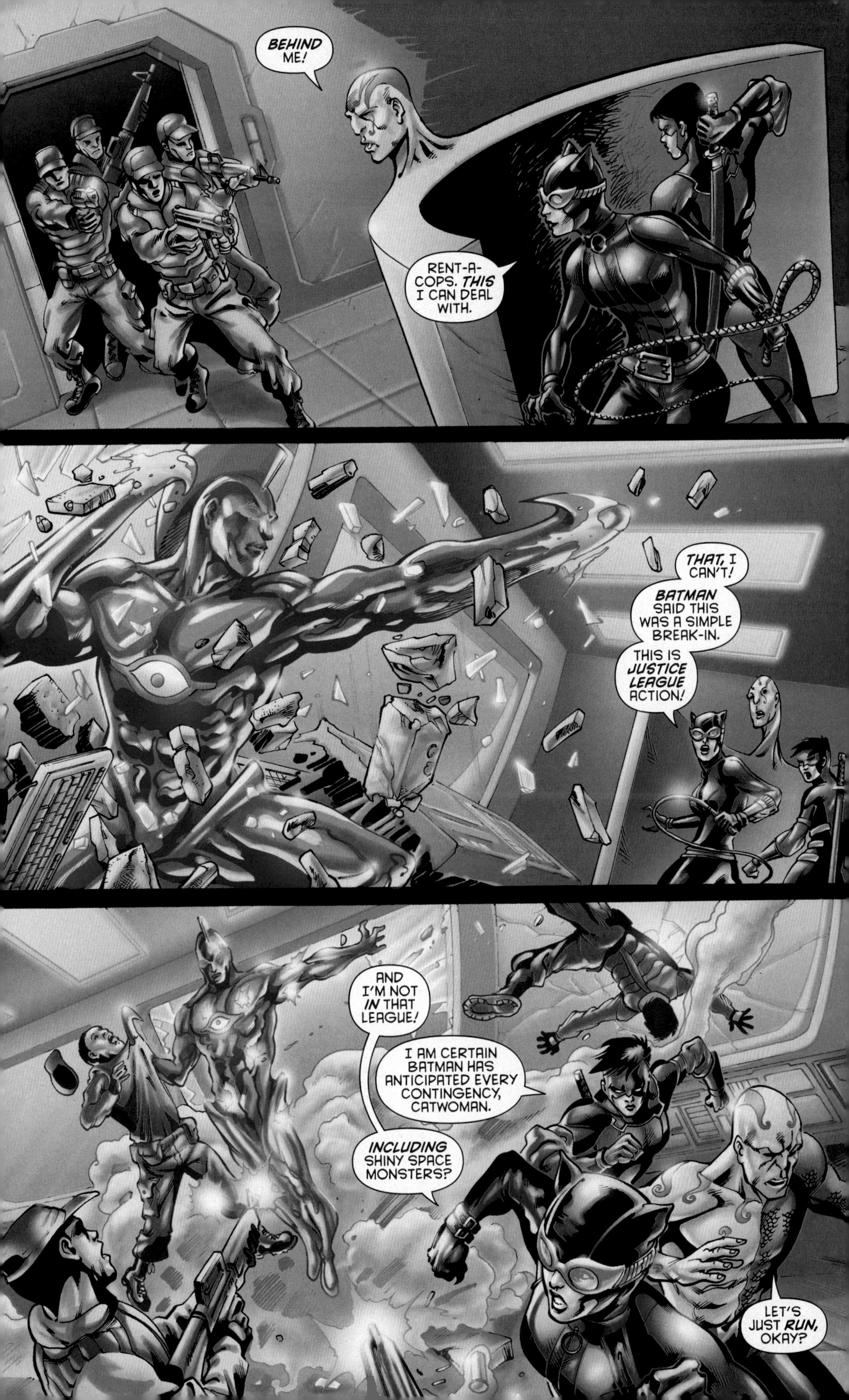
BEHIND ME!
RENT-A-COPS. THIS I CAN DEAL WITH.
THAT, I CAN'T!
BATMAN SAID THIS WAS A SIMPLE BREAK-IN.
THIS IS JUSTICE LEAGUE ACTION!
AND I'M NOT IN THAT LEAGUE!
I AM CERTAIN BATMAN HAS ANTICIPATED EVERY CONTINGENCY, CATWOMAN.
INCLUDING SHINY SPACE MONSTERS?
LET'S JUST RUN, OKAY?

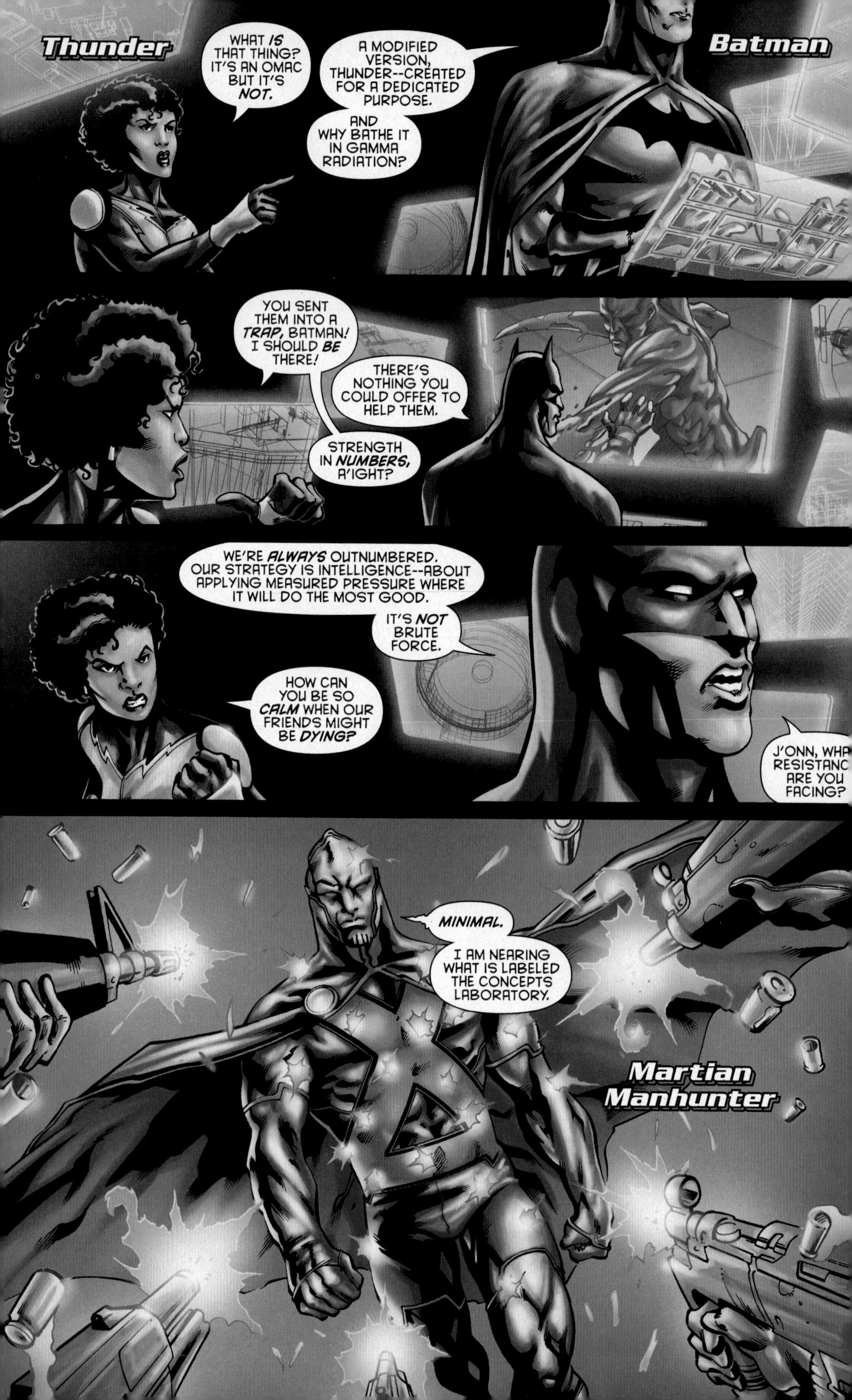
Thunder
WHAT IS THAT THING? IT'S AN OMAC BUT IT'S NOT.
Batman
A MODIFIED VERSION, THUNDER--CREATED FOR A DEDICATED PURPOSE.
AND WHY BATHE IT IN GAMMA RADIATION?
YOU SENT THEM INTO A TRAP, BATMAN! I SHOULD BE THERE!
THERE'S NOTHING YOU COULD OFFER TO HELP THEM.
STRENGTH IN NUMBERS, A'IGHT?
WE'RE ALWAYS OUTNUMBERED. OUR STRATEGY IS INTELLIGENCE--ABOUT APPLYING MEASURED PRESSURE WHERE IT WILL DO THE MOST GOOD.
IT'S NOT BRUTE FORCE.
HOW CAN YOU BE SO CALM WHEN OUR FRIENDS MIGHT BE DYING?
J'ONN, WHA RESISTANC ARE YOU FACING?
MINIMAL.
I AM NEARING WHAT IS LABELED THE CONCEPTS LABORATORY.
Martian Manhunter

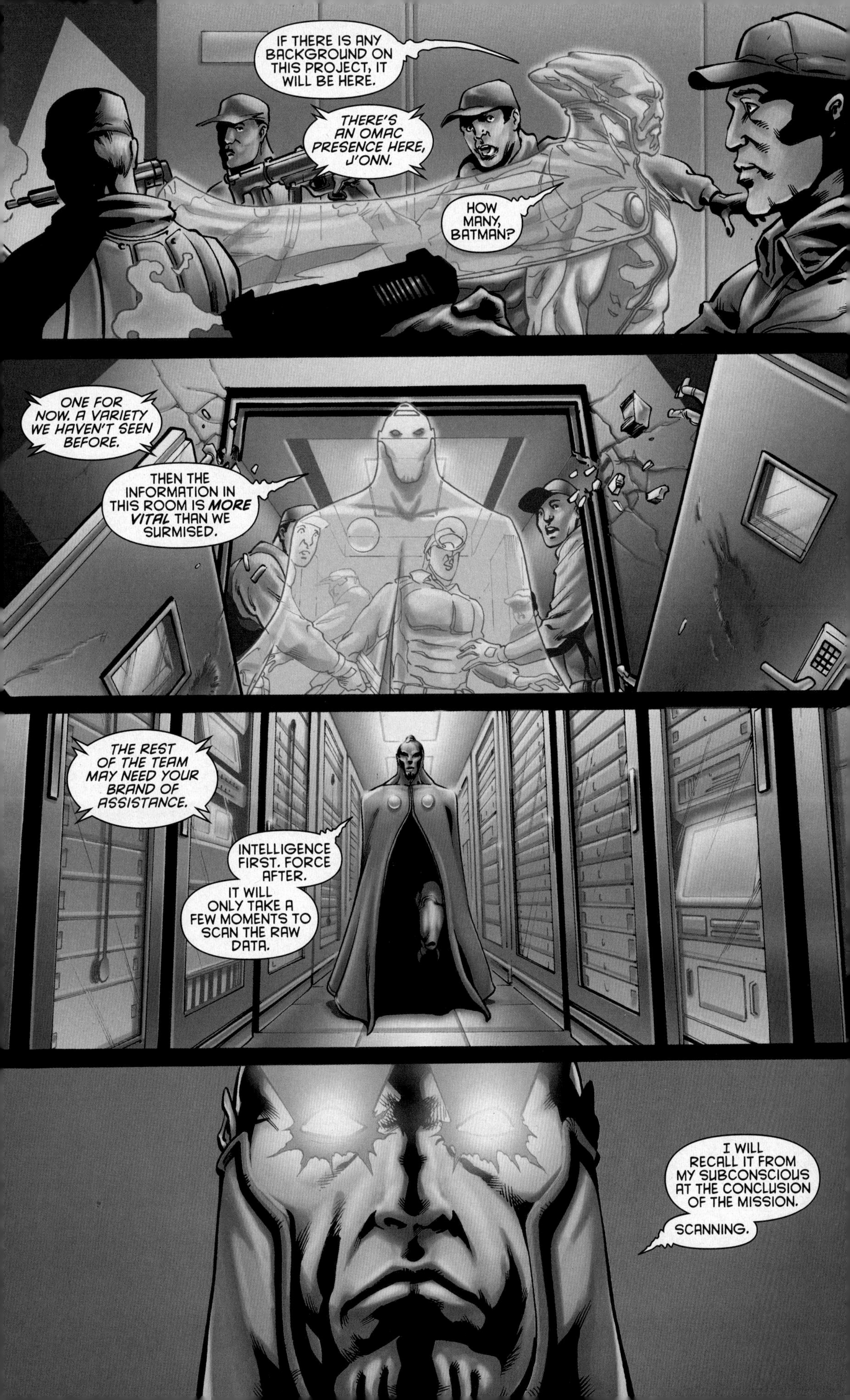
IF THERE IS ANY BACKGROUND ON THIS PROJECT, IT WILL BE HERE.
THERE'S AN OMAC PRESENCE HERE, J'ONN.
HOW MANY, BATMAN?
ONE FOR NOW. A VARIETY WE HAVEN'T SEEN BEFORE.
THEN THE INFORMATION IN THIS ROOM IS *MORE VITAL* THAN WE SURMISED.
THE REST OF THE TEAM MAY NEED YOUR BRAND OF ASSISTANCE.
INTELLIGENCE FIRST. FORCE AFTER.
IT WILL ONLY TAKE A FEW MOMENTS TO SCAN THE RAW DATA.
I WILL RECALL IT FROM MY SUBCONSCIOUS AT THE CONCLUSION OF THE MISSION.
SCANNING.

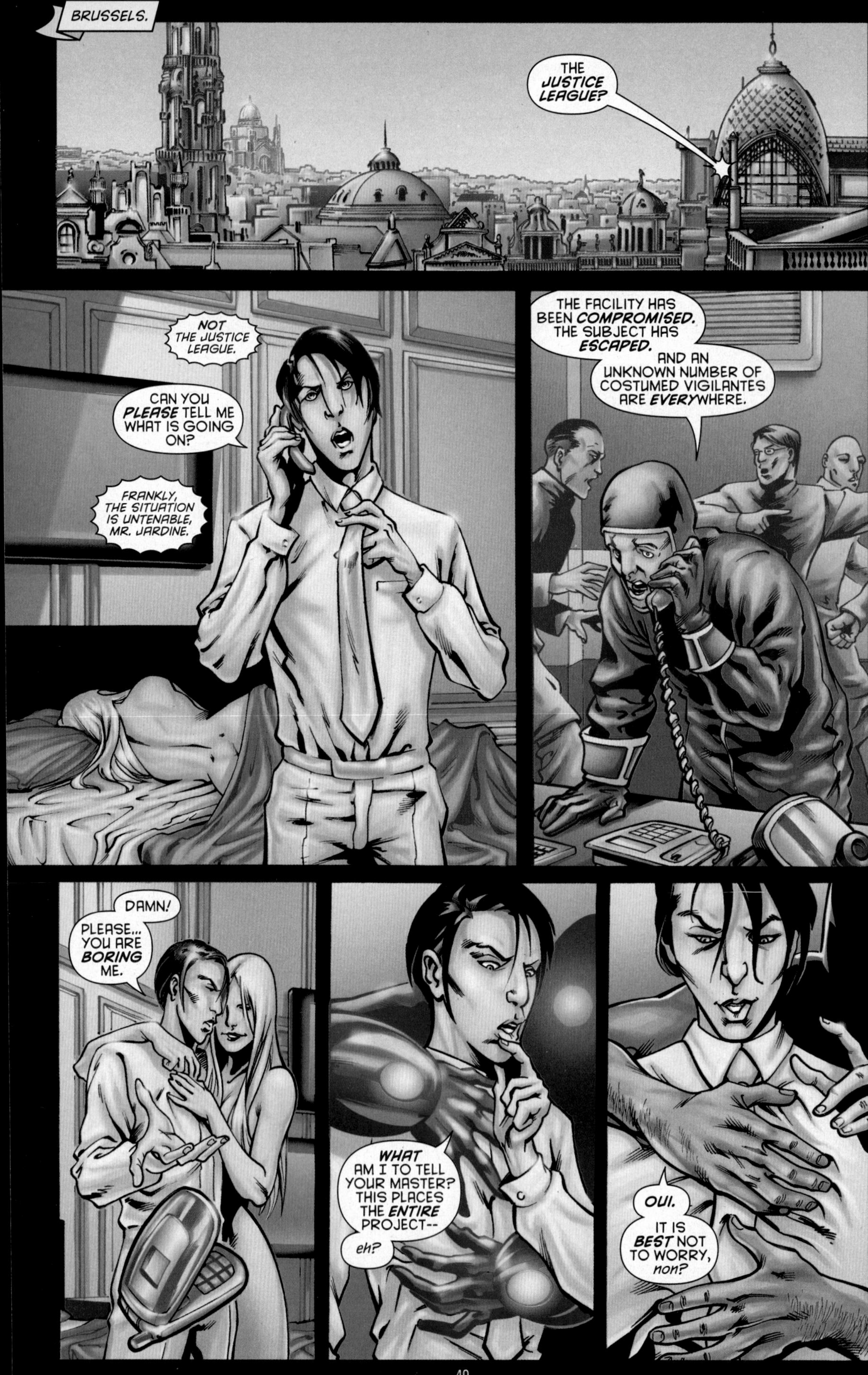
BRUSSELS.
THE JUSTICE LEAGUE?
NOT THE JUSTICE LEAGUE.
CAN YOU PLEASE TELL ME WHAT IS GOING ON?
FRANKLY, THE SITUATION IS UNTENABLE, MR. JARDINE.
THE FACILITY HAS BEEN COMPROMISED. THE SUBJECT HAS ESCAPED.
AND AN UNKNOWN NUMBER OF COSTUMED VIGILANTES ARE EVERYWHERE.
DAMN!
PLEASE... YOU ARE BORING ME.
WHAT AM I TO TELL YOUR MASTER? THIS PLACES THE ENTIRE PROJECT--
eh?
OUI.
IT IS BEST NOT TO WORRY, non?

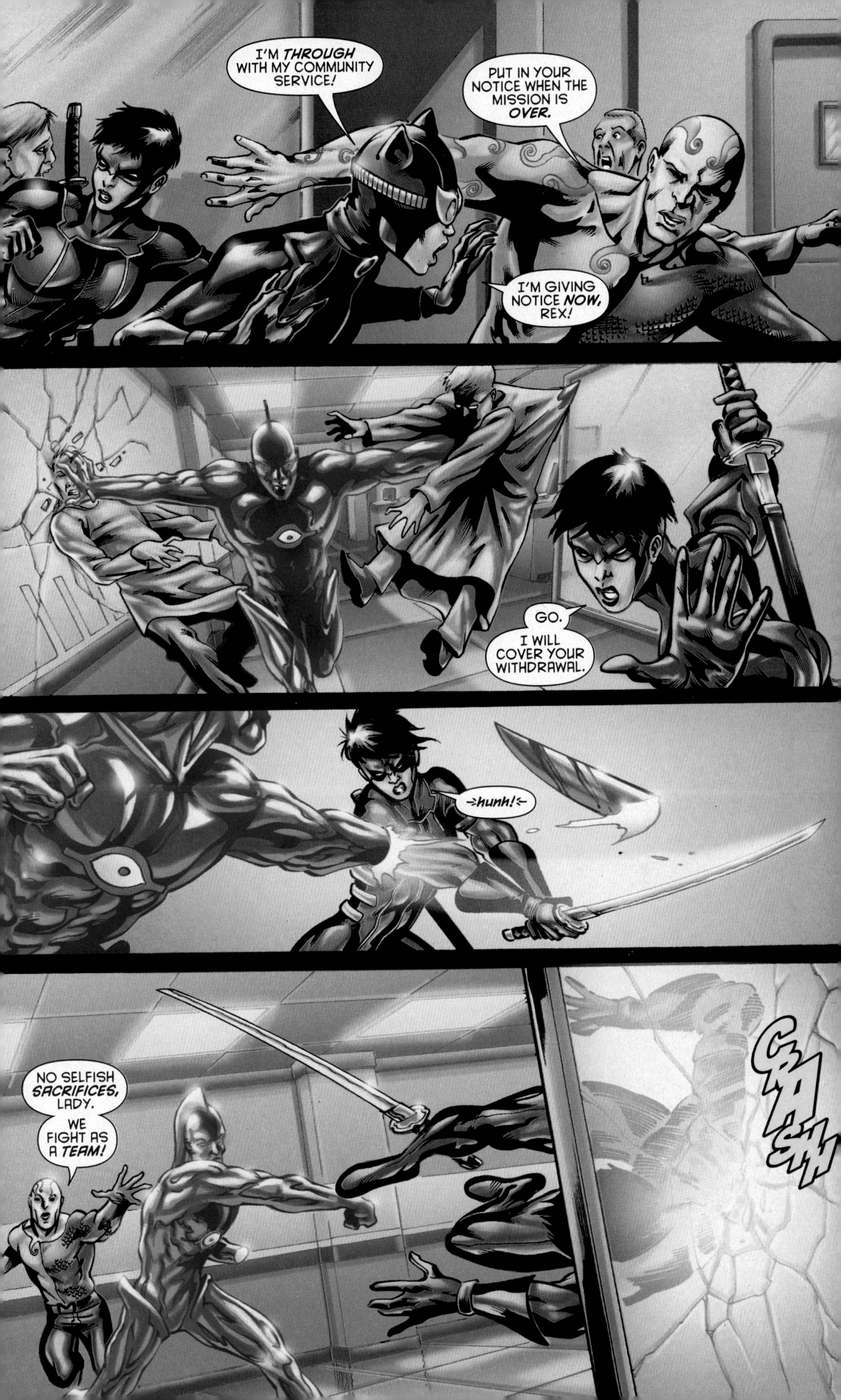
I'M THROUGH WITH MY COMMUNITY SERVICE!
PUT IN YOUR NOTICE WHEN THE MISSION IS OVER.
I'M GIVING NOTICE NOW, REX!
GO. I WILL COVER YOUR WITHDRAWAL.
hunh!
NO SELFISH SACRIFICES, LADY.
WE FIGHT AS A TEAM!
CRASH

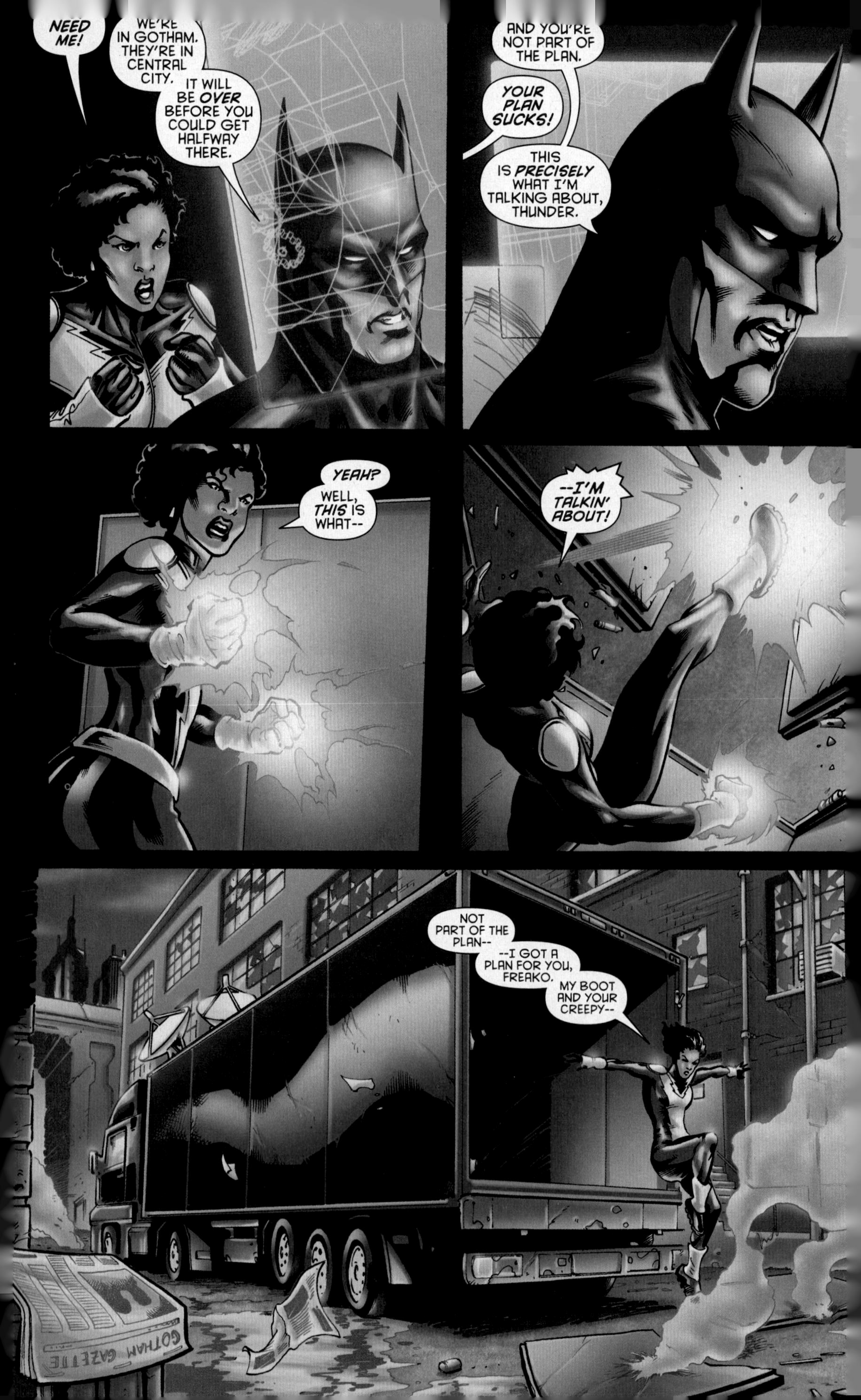
NEED ME!
WE'RE IN GOTHAM. THEY'RE IN CENTRAL CITY.
IT WILL BE OVER BEFORE YOU COULD GET HALFWAY THERE.
AND YOU'RE NOT PART OF THE PLAN.
YOUR PLAN SUCKS!
THIS IS PRECISELY WHAT I'M TALKING ABOUT, THUNDER.
YEAH?
WELL, THIS IS WHAT--
--I'M TALKIN' ABOUT!
NOT PART OF THE PLAN--
--I GOT A PLAN FOR YOU, FREAKO.
MY BOOT AND YOUR CREEPY--
GOTHAM GAZETTE

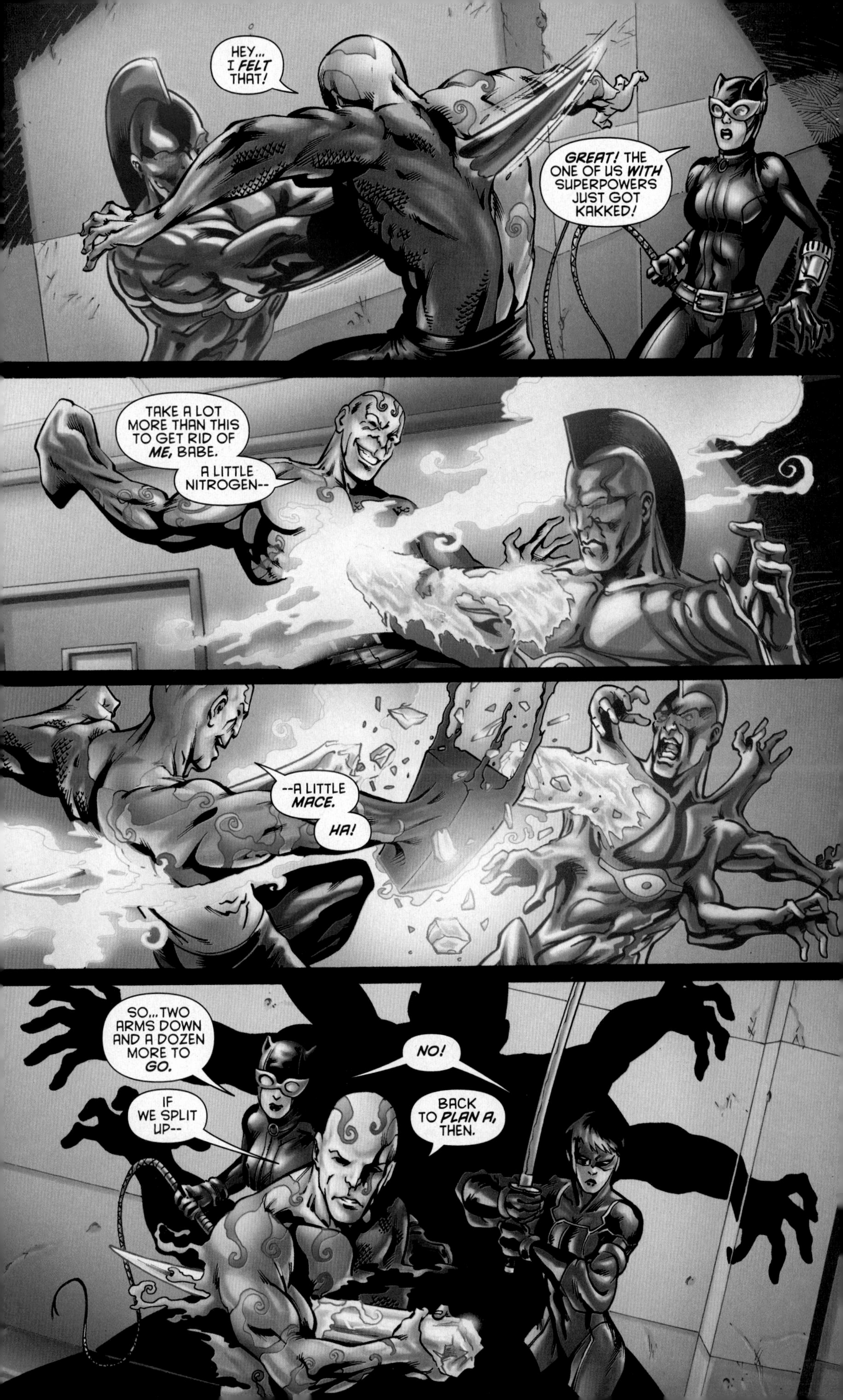
HEY... I FELT THAT!
GREAT! THE ONE OF US WITH SUPERPOWERS JUST GOT KAKKED!
TAKE A LOT MORE THAN THIS TO GET RID OF ME, BABE.
A LITTLE NITROGEN--
--A LITTLE MACE.
HA!
SO... TWO ARMS DOWN AND A DOZEN MORE TO GO.
IF WE SPLIT UP--
NO!
BACK TO PLAN A, THEN.

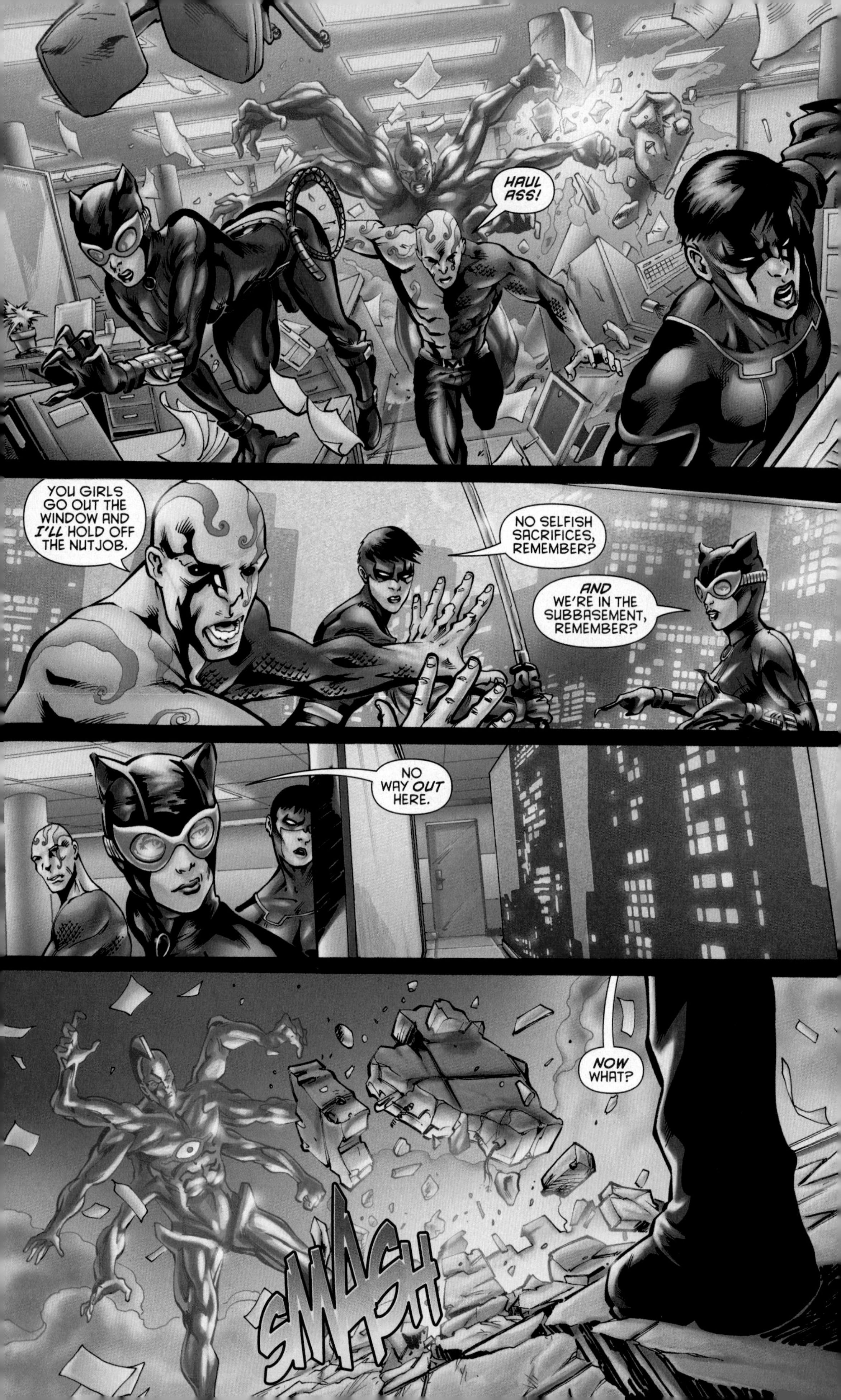
HAUL ASS!
YOU GIRLS GO OUT THE WINDOW AND I'LL HOLD OFF THE NUTJOB.
NO SELFISH SACRIFICES, REMEMBER?
AND WE'RE IN THE SUBBASEMENT, REMEMBER?
NO WAY OUT HERE.
NOW WHAT?
SMASH

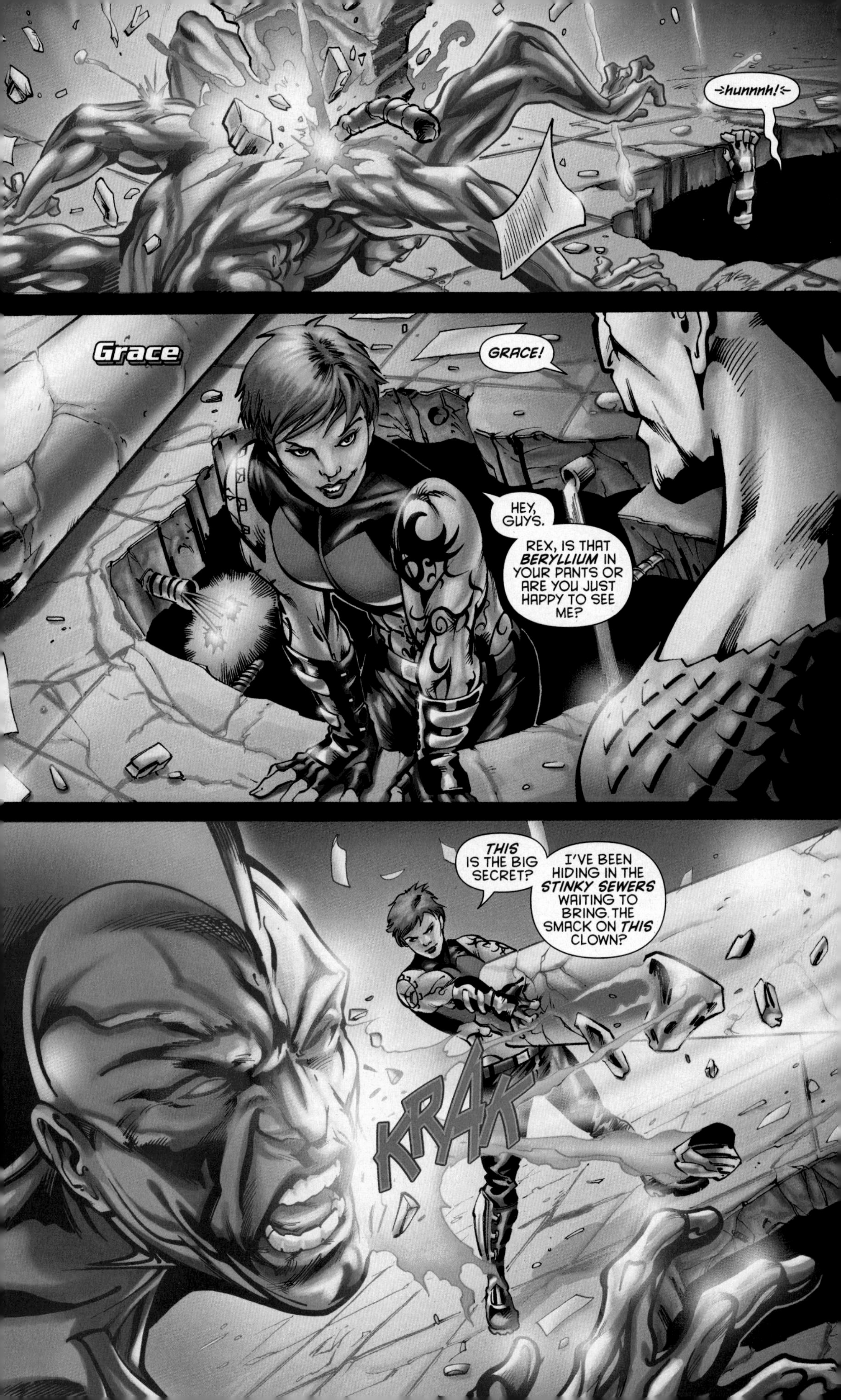

hunnnh!
Grace
GRACE!
HEY, GUYS.
REX, IS THAT BERYLLIUM IN YOUR PANTS OR ARE YOU JUST HAPPY TO SEE ME?
THIS IS THE BIG SECRET?
I'VE BEEN HIDING IN THE STINKY SEWERS WAITING TO BRING THE SMACK ON THIS CLOWN?
KRAK

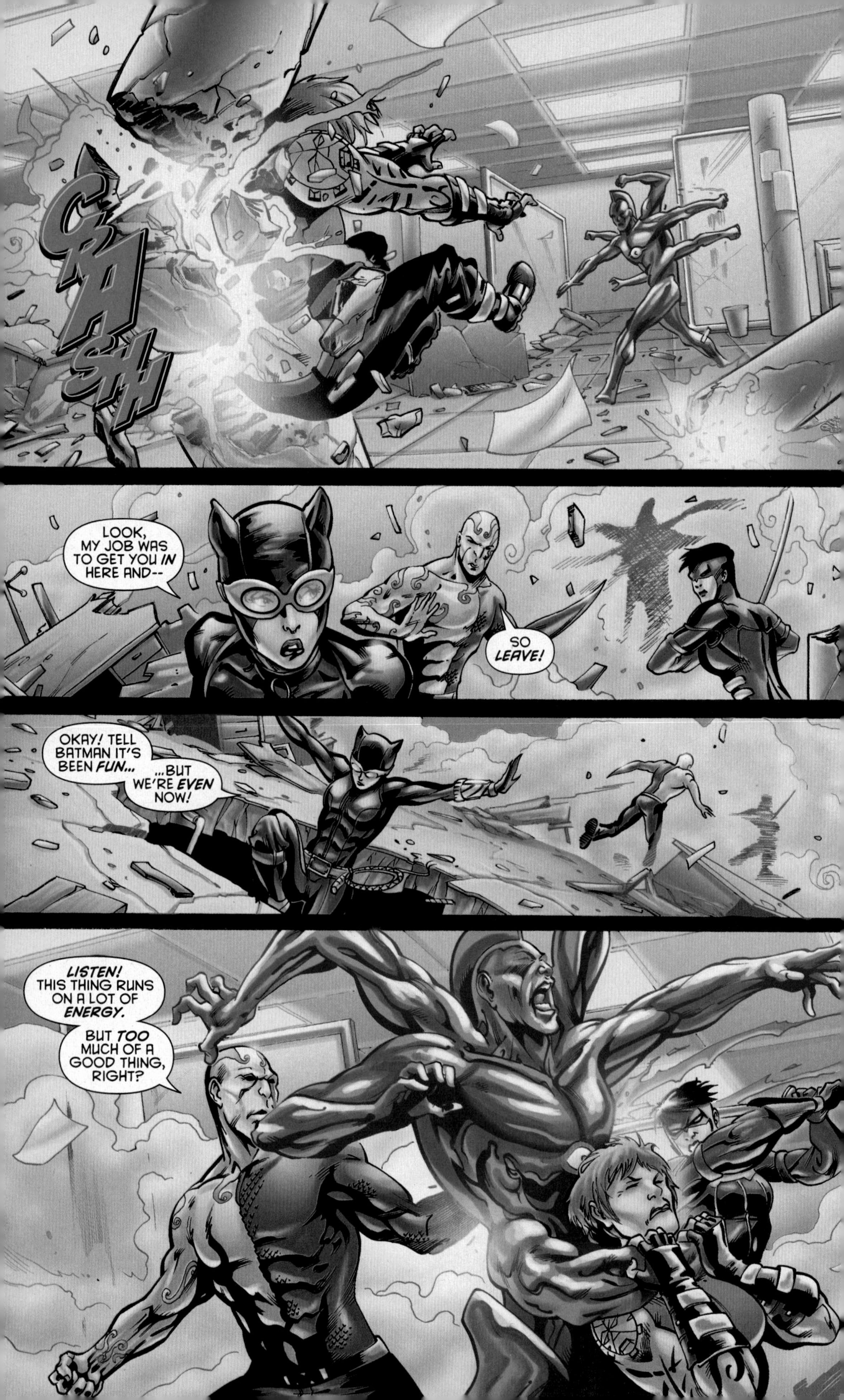
CRASH
LOOK, MY JOB WAS TO GET YOU IN HERE AND--
SO LEAVE!
OKAY! TELL BATMAN IT'S BEEN FUN...
...BUT WE'RE EVEN NOW!
LISTEN! THIS THING RUNS ON A LOT OF ENERGY.
BUT TOO MUCH OF A GOOD THING, RIGHT?

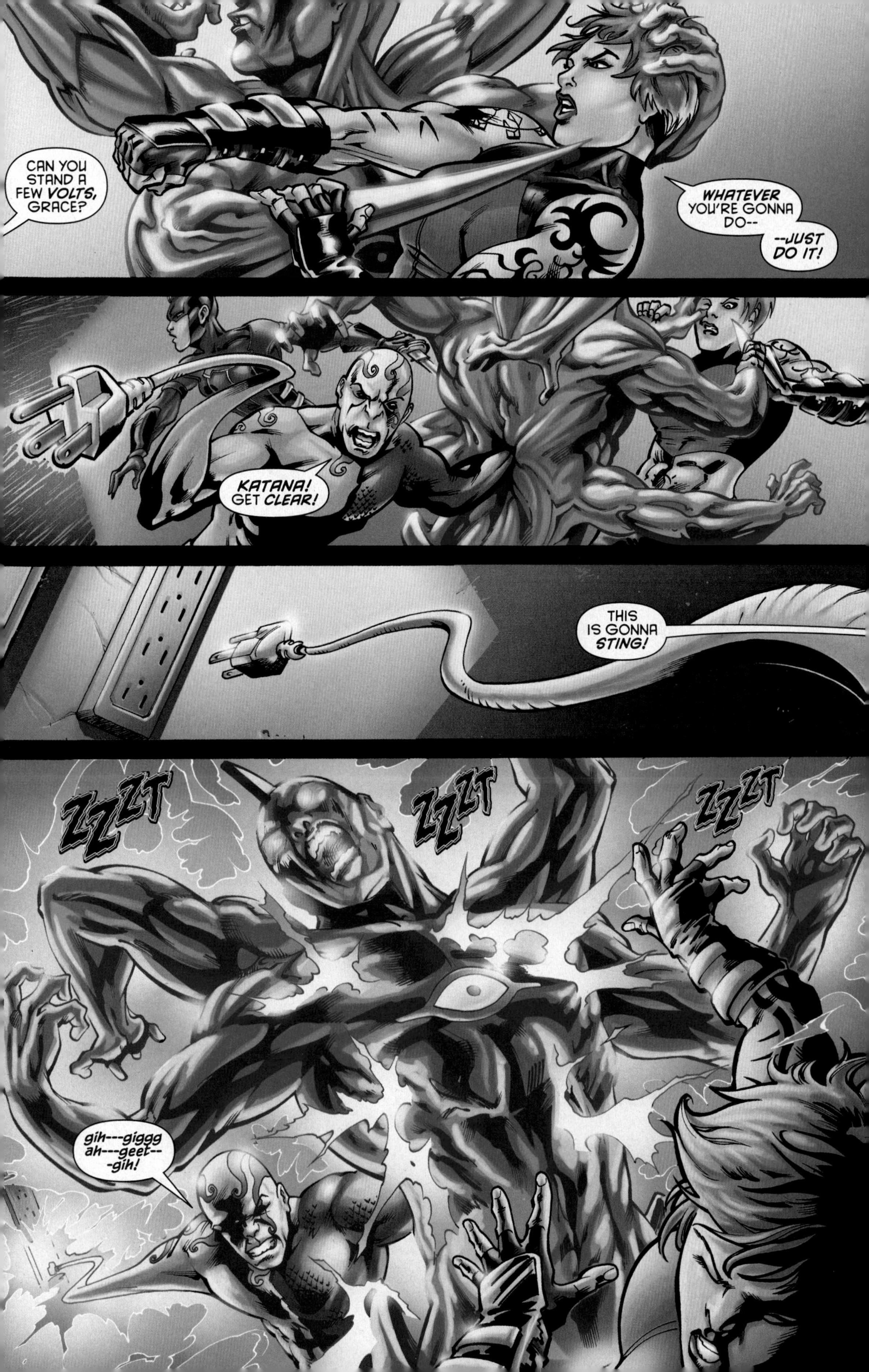
CAN YOU STAND A FEW VOLTS, GRACE?
WHATEVER YOU'RE GONNA DO--
--JUST DO IT!
KATANA! GET CLEAR!
THIS IS GONNA STING!
ZZZZT
ZZZZT
ZZZZT
gih---giggg ah---geet-- -gih!

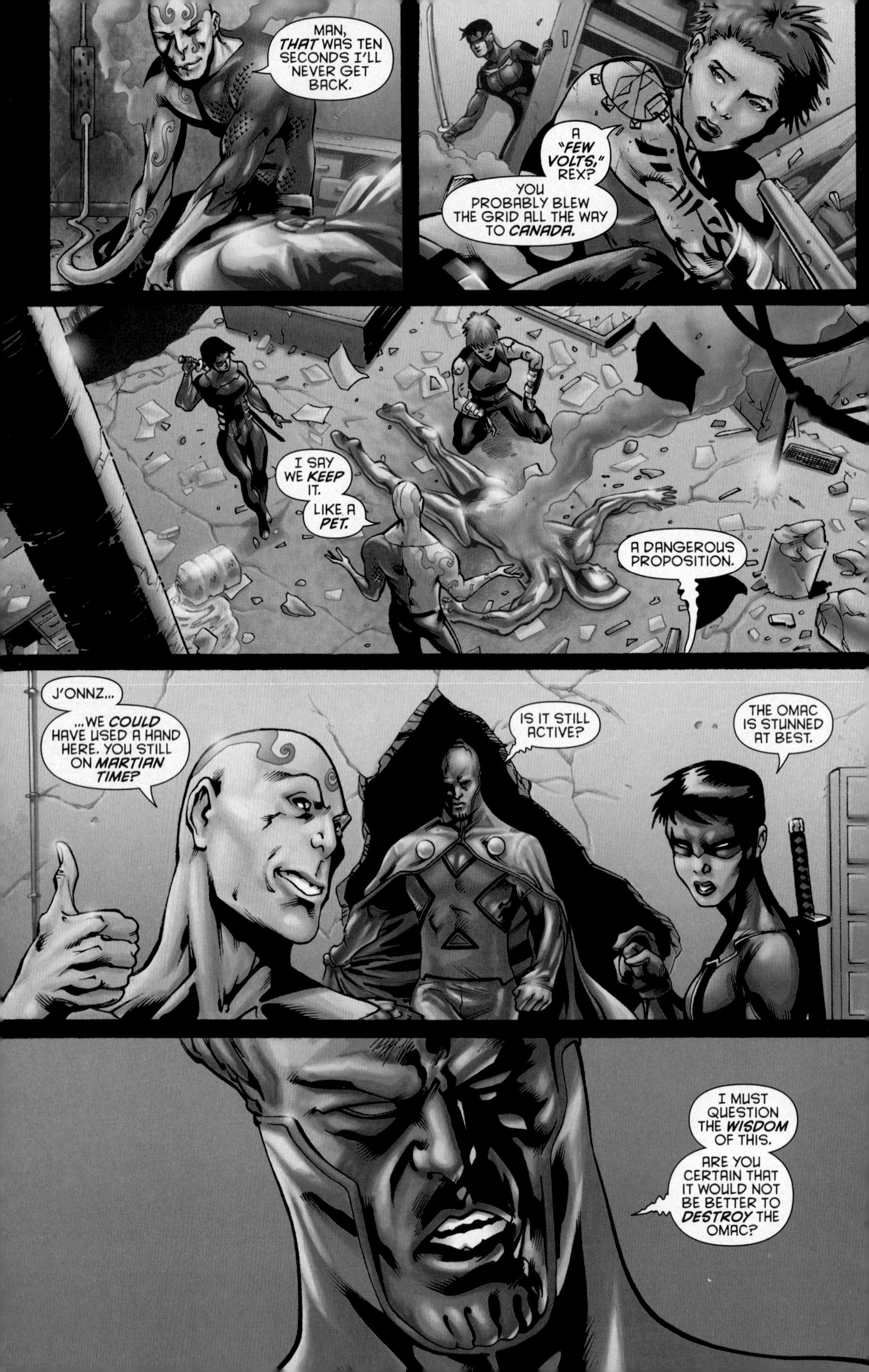
MAN, THAT WAS TEN SECONDS I'LL NEVER GET BACK.
A "FEW VOLTS," REX?
YOU PROBABLY BLEW THE GRID ALL THE WAY TO CANADA.
I SAY WE KEEP IT.
LIKE A PET.
A DANGEROUS PROPOSITION.
J'ONNZ...
...WE COULD HAVE USED A HAND HERE. YOU STILL ON MARTIAN TIME?
IS IT STILL ACTIVE?
THE OMAC IS STUNNED AT BEST.
I MUST QUESTION THE WISDOM OF THIS.
ARE YOU CERTAIN THAT IT WOULD NOT BE BETTER TO DESTROY THE OMAC?

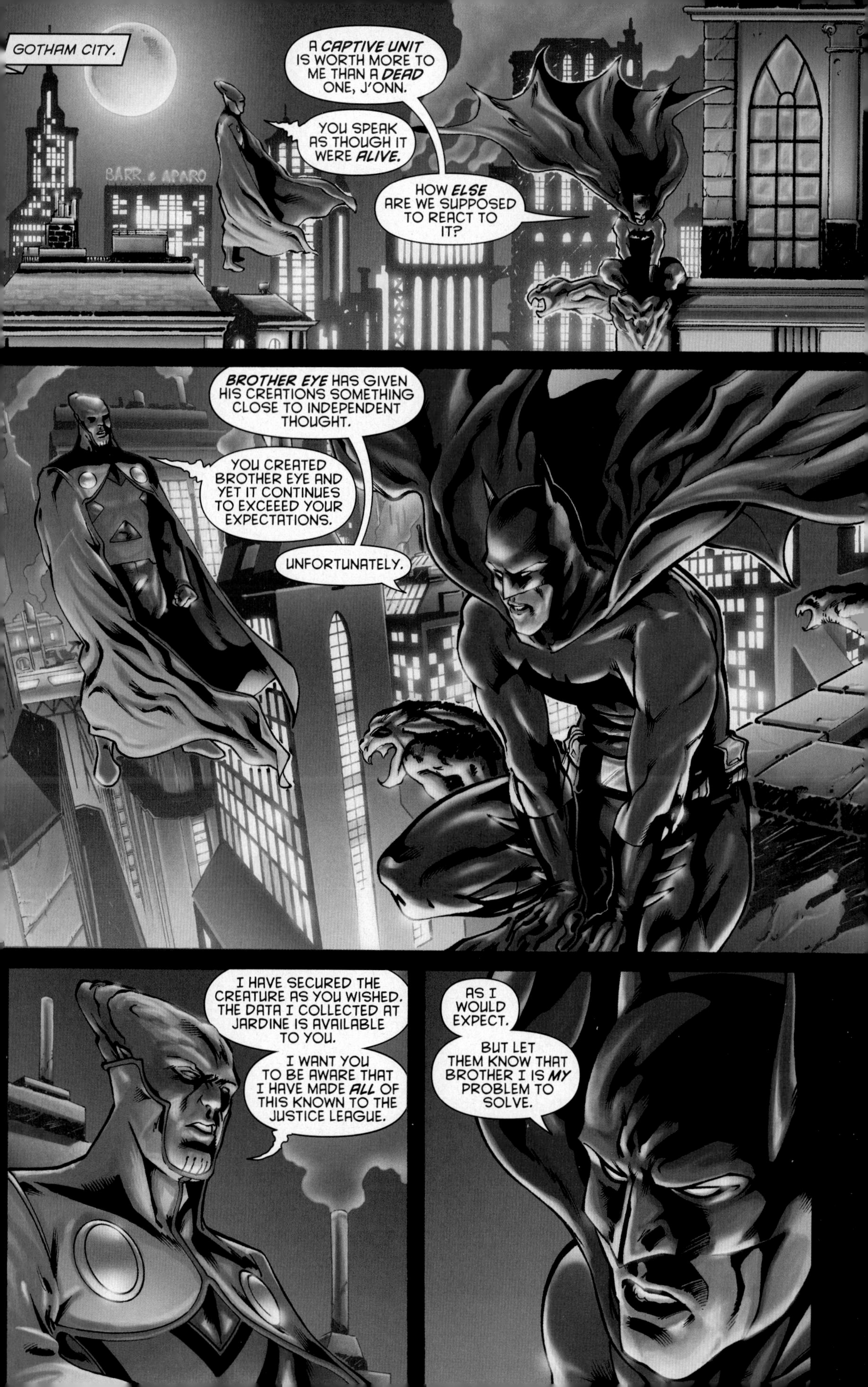
GOTHAM CITY.
A CAPTIVE UNIT IS WORTH MORE TO ME THAN A DEAD ONE, J'ONN.
YOU SPEAK AS THOUGH IT WERE ALIVE.
HOW ELSE ARE WE SUPPOSED TO REACT TO IT?
BARR. & APARO
BROTHER EYE HAS GIVEN HIS CREATIONS SOMETHING CLOSE TO INDEPENDENT THOUGHT.
YOU CREATED BROTHER EYE AND YET IT CONTINUES TO EXCEED YOUR EXPECTATIONS.
UNFORTUNATELY.
I HAVE SECURED THE CREATURE AS YOU WISHED. THE DATA I COLLECTED AT JARDINE IS AVAILABLE TO YOU.
I WANT YOU TO BE AWARE THAT I HAVE MADE ALL OF THIS KNOWN TO THE JUSTICE LEAGUE.
AS I WOULD EXPECT.
BUT LET THEM KNOW THAT BROTHER I IS MY PROBLEM TO SOLVE.

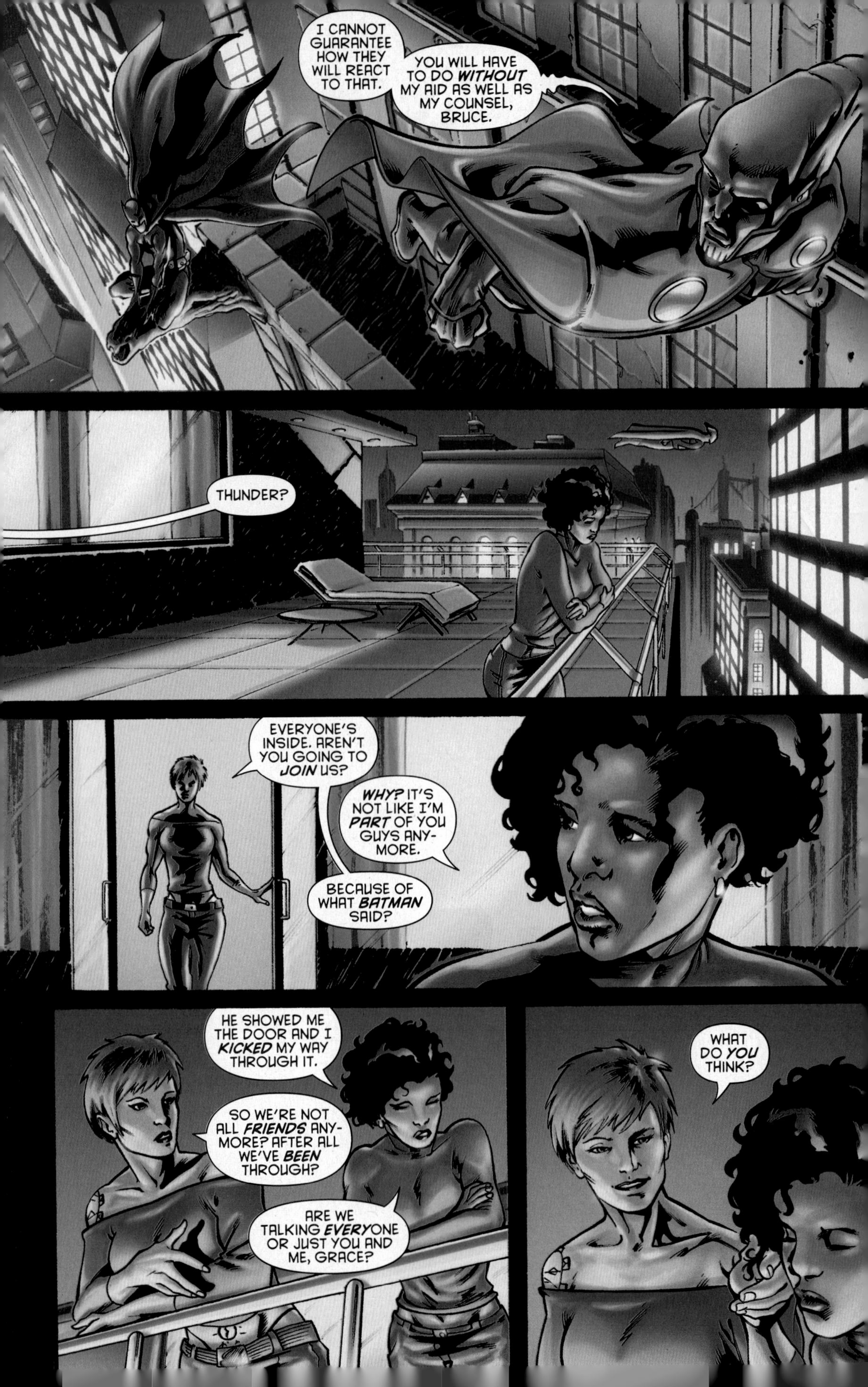
I CANNOT GUARANTEE HOW THEY WILL REACT TO THAT.
YOU WILL HAVE TO DO WITHOUT MY AID AS WELL AS MY COUNSEL, BRUCE.
THUNDER?
EVERYONE'S INSIDE. AREN'T YOU GOING TO JOIN US?
WHY? IT'S NOT LIKE I'M PART OF YOU GUYS ANY-MORE.
BECAUSE OF WHAT BATMAN SAID?
HE SHOWED ME THE DOOR AND I KICKED MY WAY THROUGH IT.
SO WE'RE NOT ALL FRIENDS ANY-MORE? AFTER ALL WE'VE BEEN THROUGH?
ARE WE TALKING EVERYONE OR JUST YOU AND ME, GRACE?
WHAT DO YOU THINK?

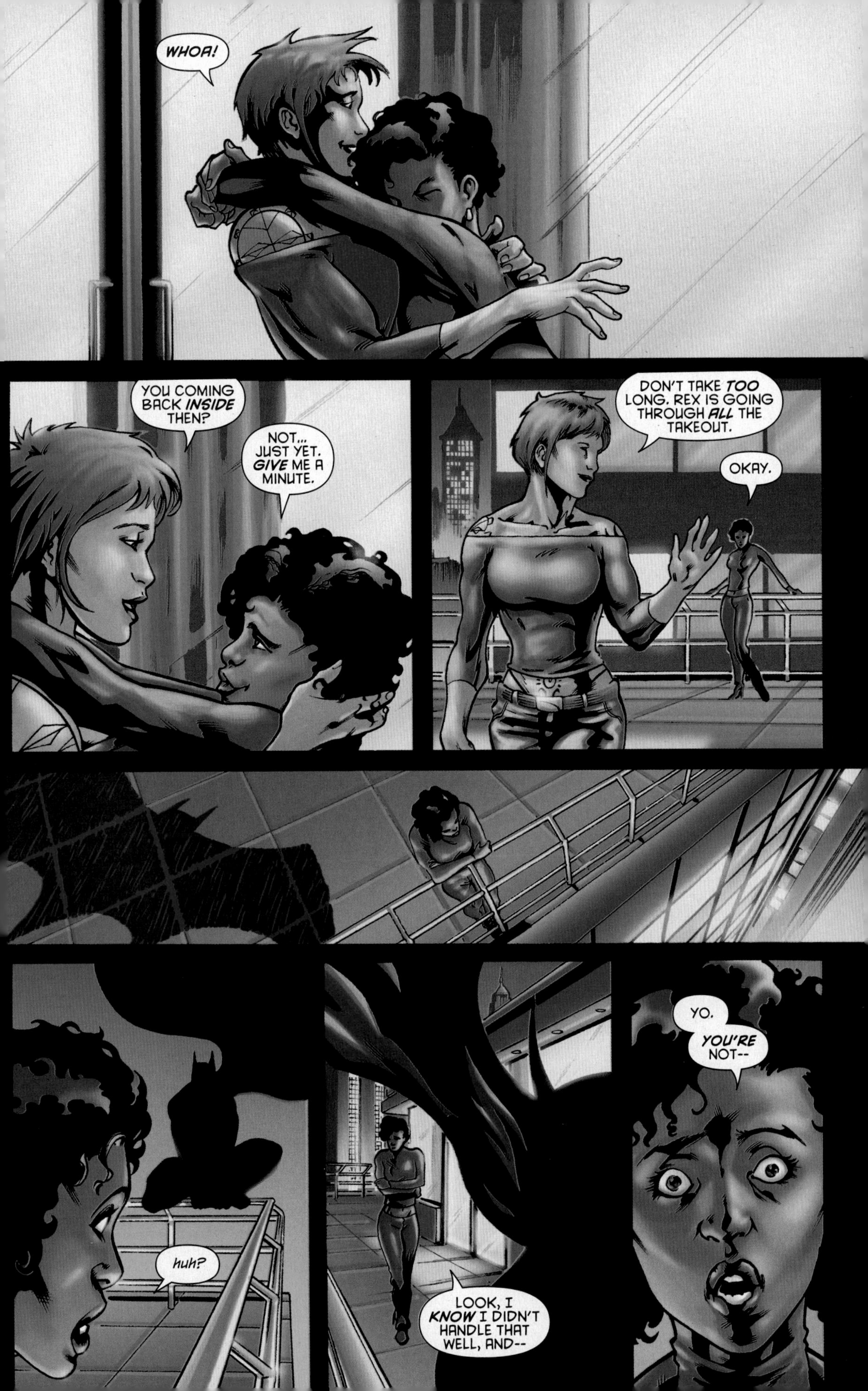
WHOA!
YOU COMING BACK INSIDE THEN?
NOT... JUST YET. GIVE ME A MINUTE.
DON'T TAKE TOO LONG. REX IS GOING THROUGH ALL THE TAKEOUT.
OKAY.
huh?
LOOK, I KNOW I DIDN'T HANDLE THAT WELL, AND--
YO.
YOU'RE NOT--

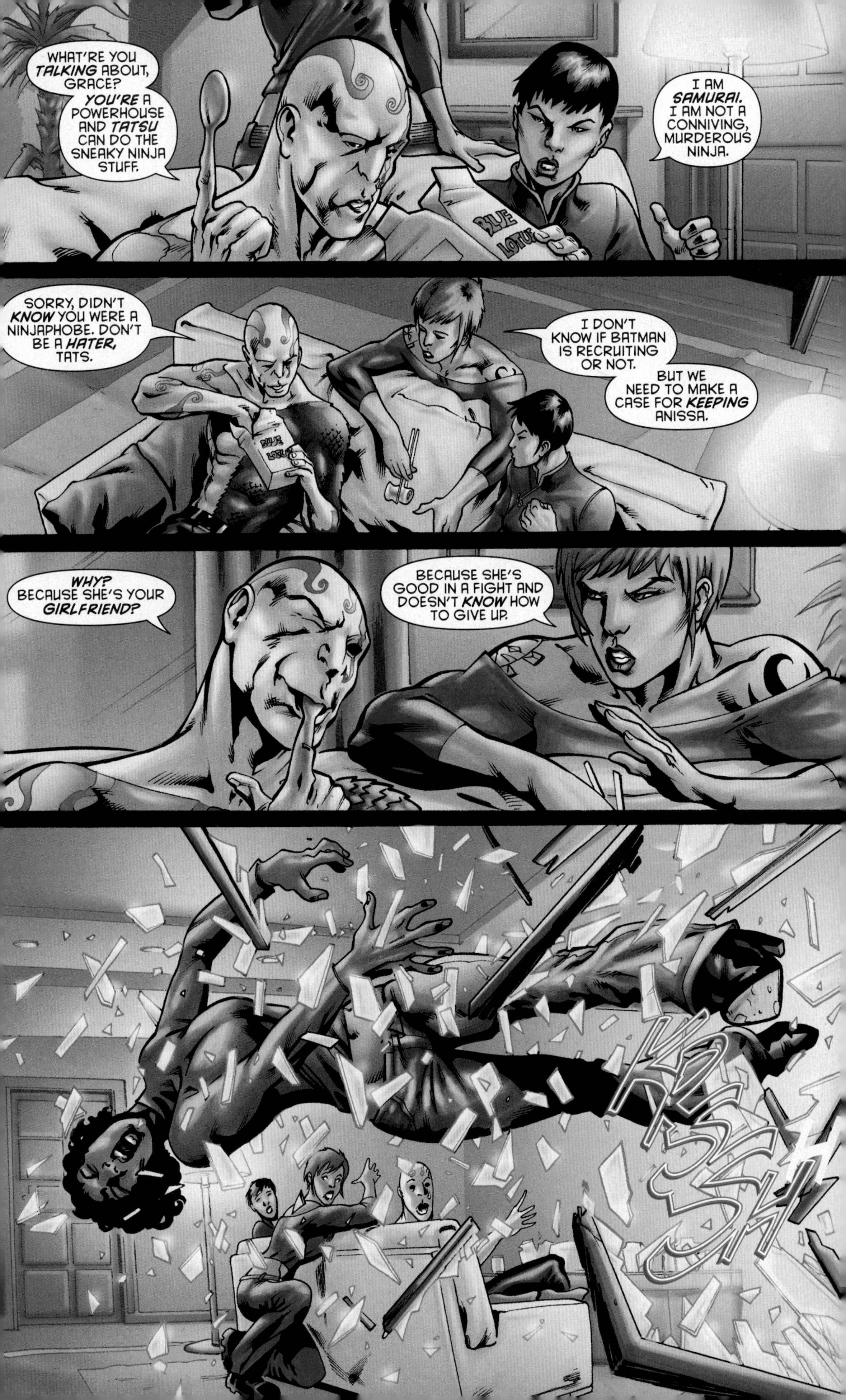
WHAT'RE YOU TALKING ABOUT, GRACE? YOU'RE A POWERHOUSE AND TATSU CAN DO THE SNEAKY NINJA STUFF.
I AM SAMURAI. I AM NOT A CONNIVING, MURDEROUS NINJA.
SORRY, DIDN'T KNOW YOU WERE A NINJAPHOBE. DON'T BE A HATER, TATS.
I DON'T KNOW IF BATMAN IS RECRUITING OR NOT.
BUT WE NEED TO MAKE A CASE FOR KEEPING ANISSA.
WHY? BECAUSE SHE'S YOUR GIRLFRIEND?
BECAUSE SHE'S GOOD IN A FIGHT AND DOESN'T KNOW HOW TO GIVE UP.
KRSSSHH

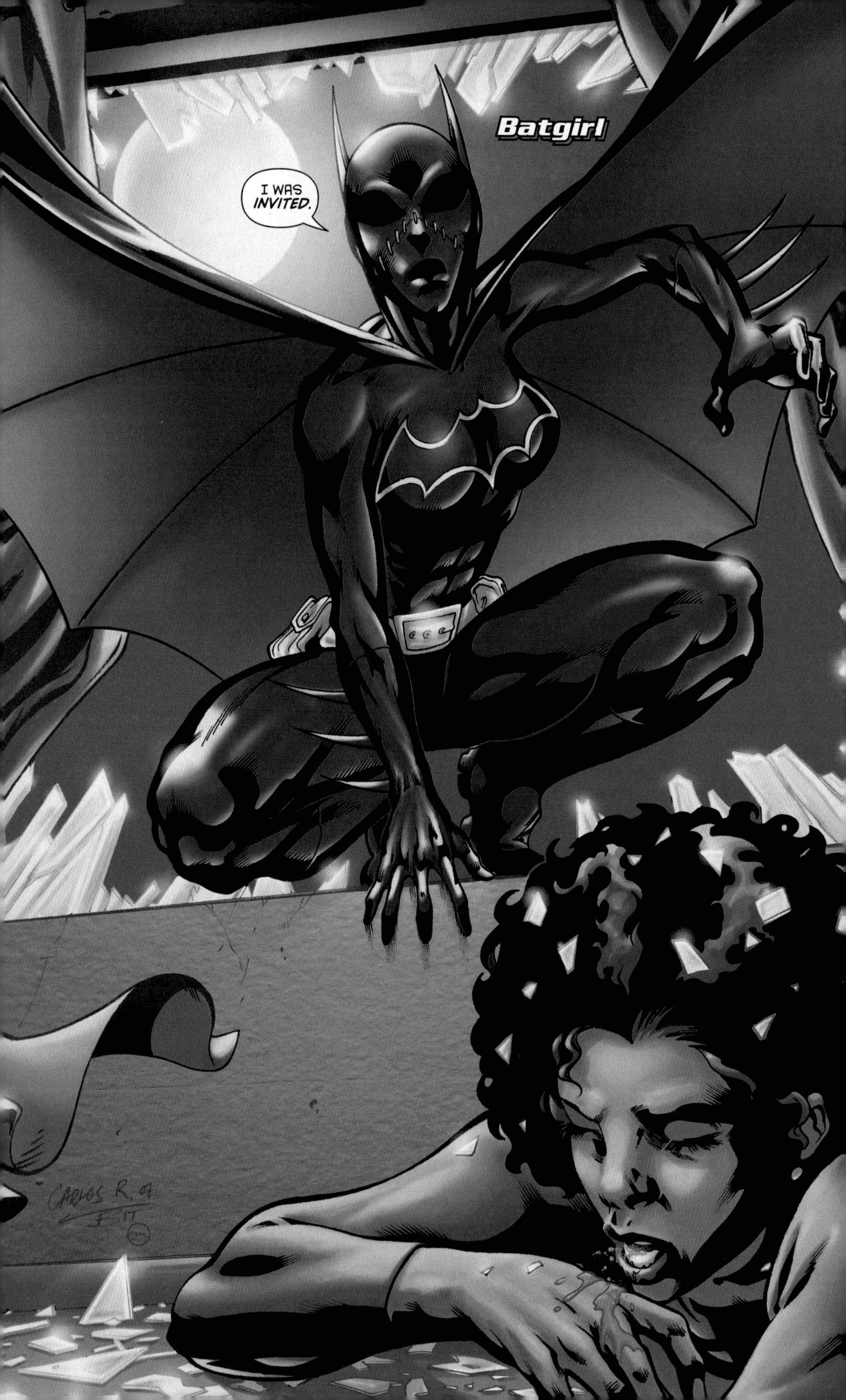
Batgirl
I WAS INVITED.

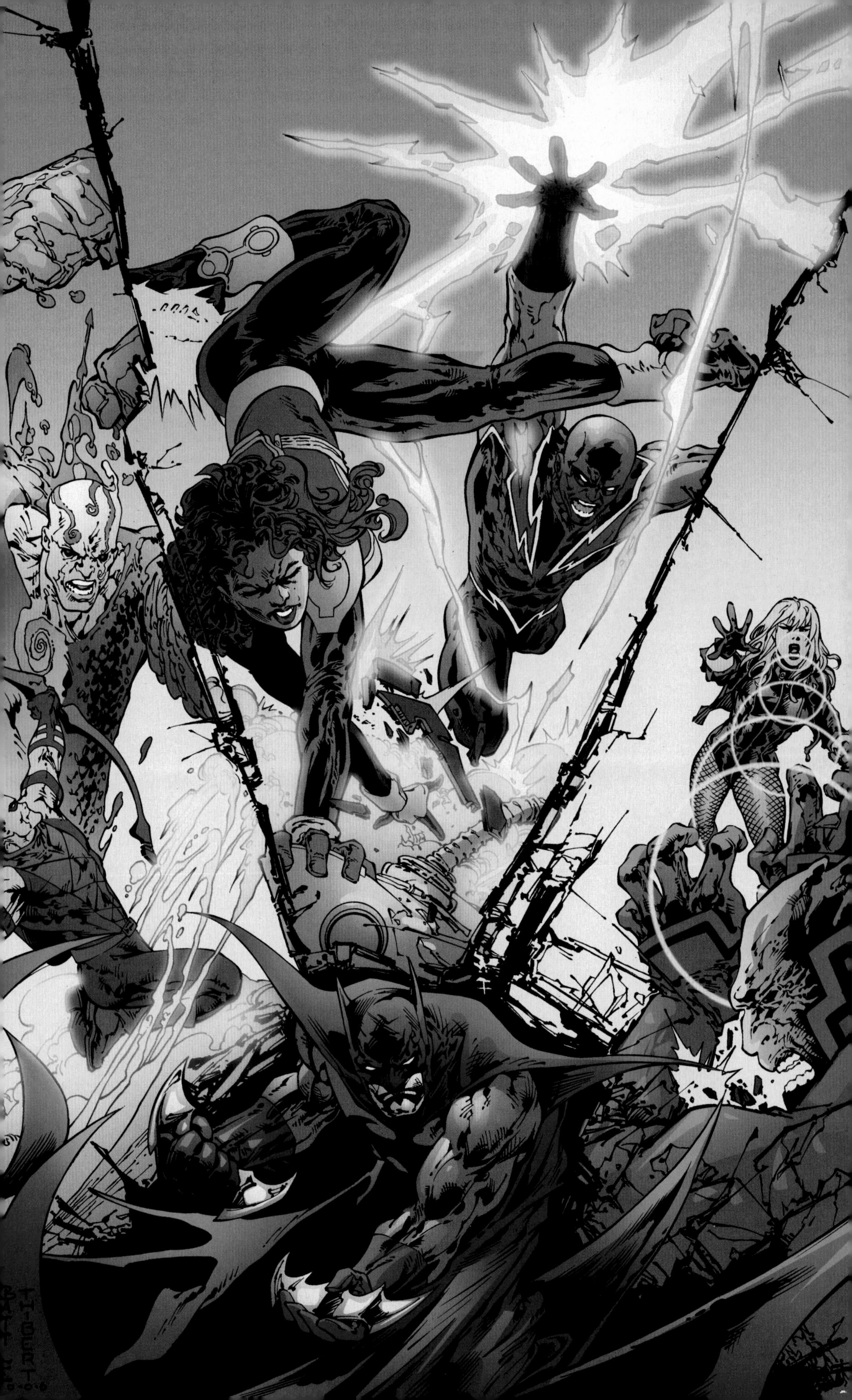

part THREE

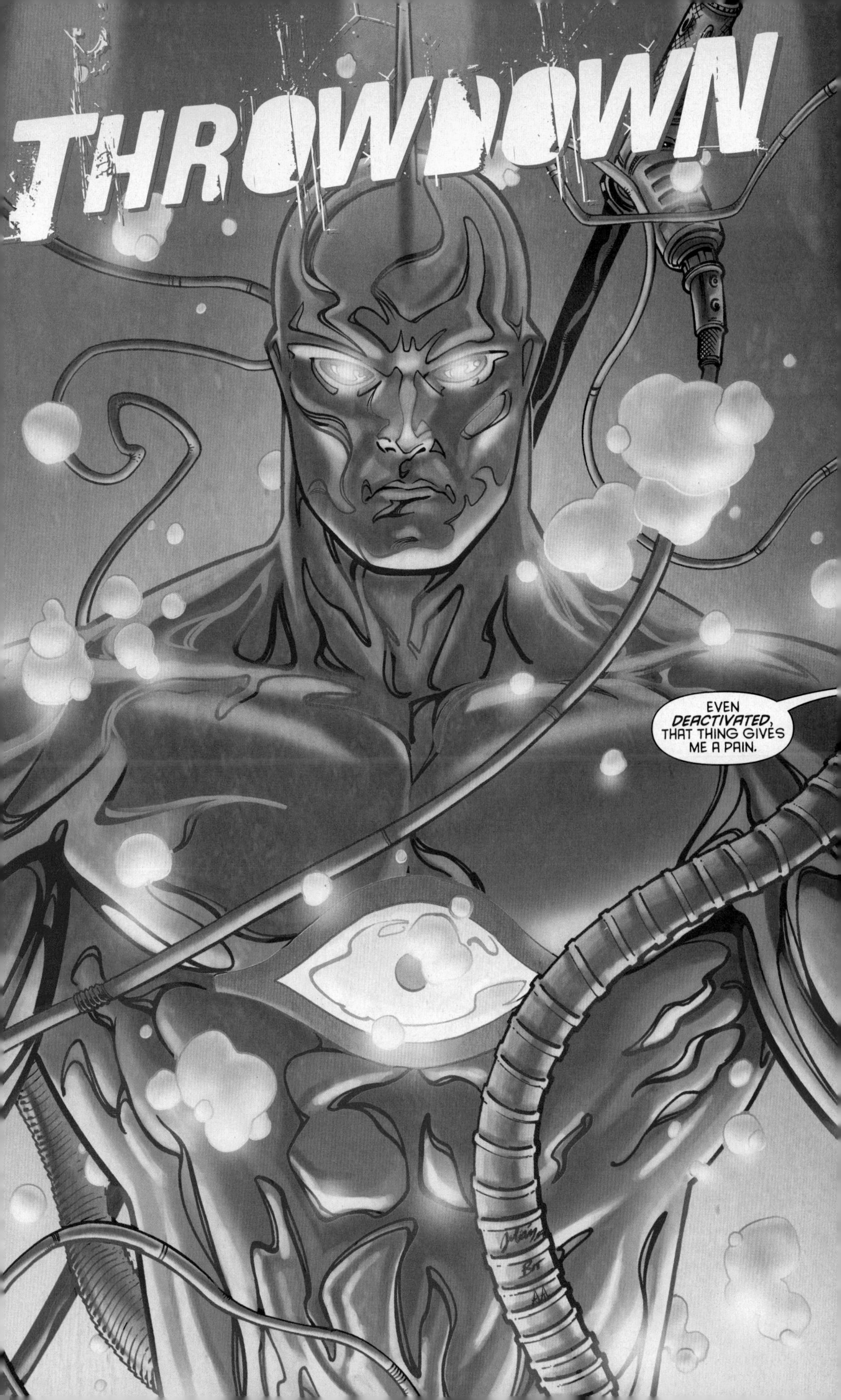
THROWDOWN
EVEN *DEACTIVATED*, THAT THING GIVES ME A PAIN.

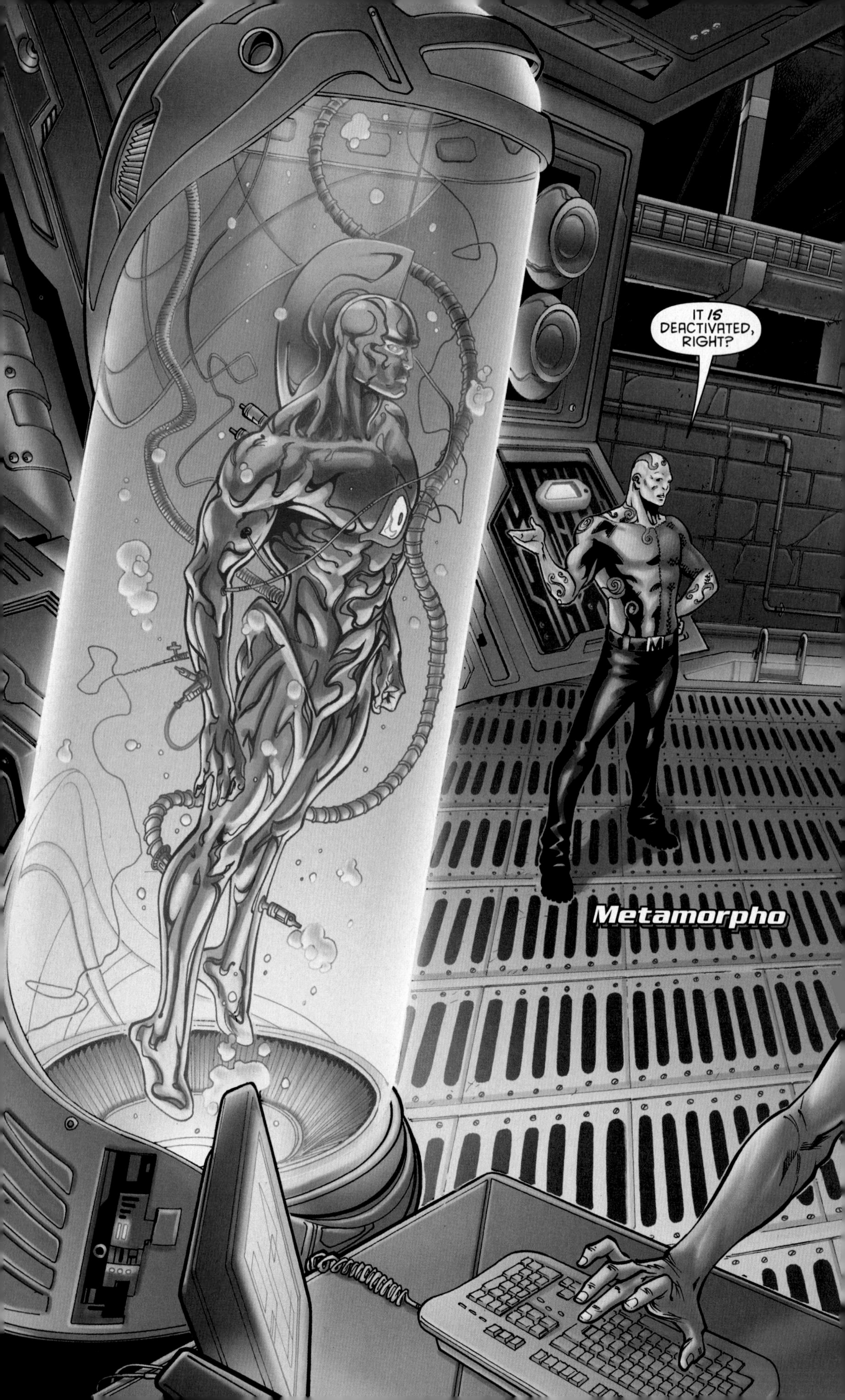
IT *IS* DEACTIVATED, RIGHT?
Metamorpho

Hawkgirl

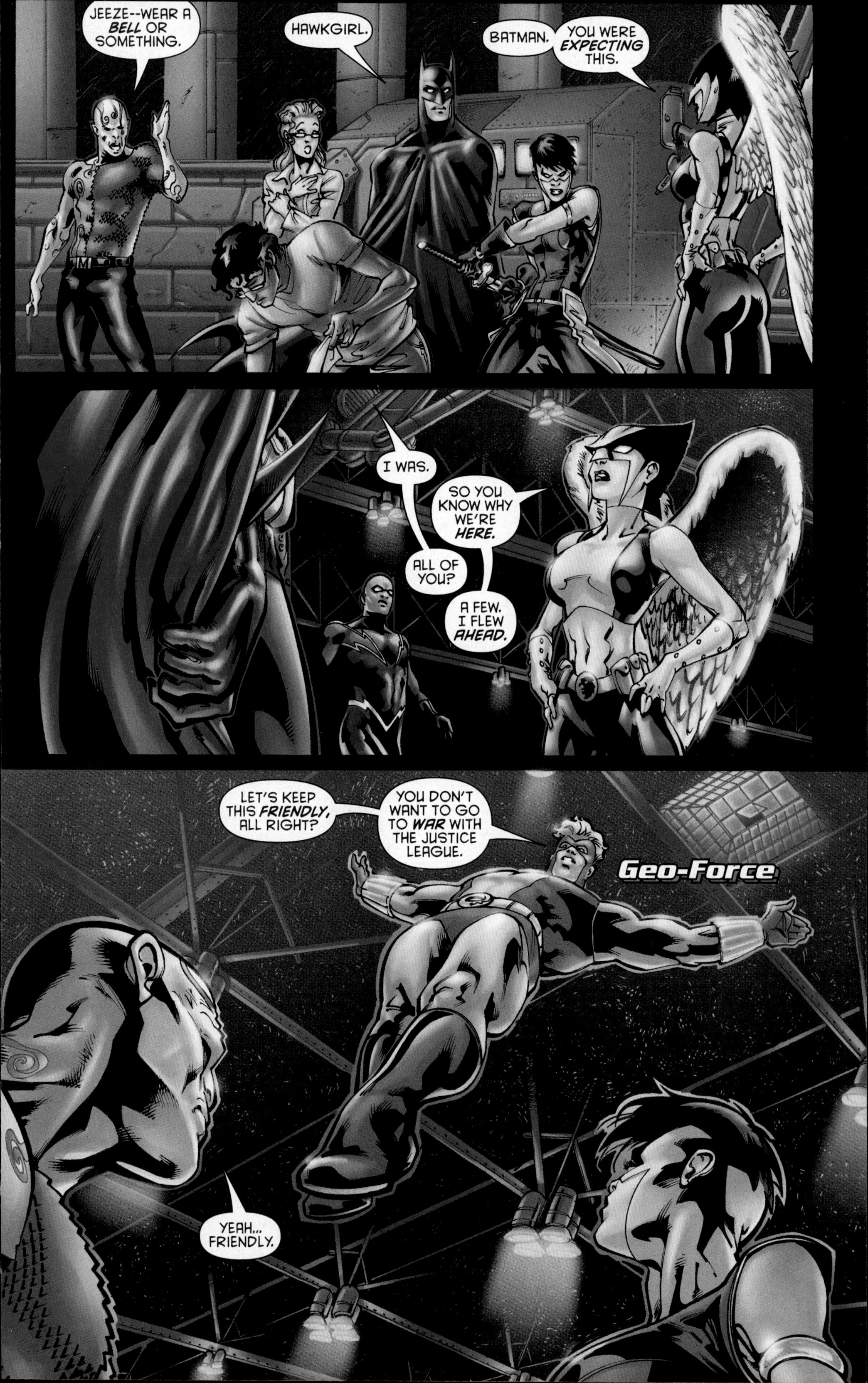
JEEZE--WEAR A BELL OR SOMETHING.
HAWKGIRL.
BATMAN.
YOU WERE EXPECTING THIS.
I WAS.
SO YOU KNOW WHY WE'RE HERE.
ALL OF YOU?
A FEW. I FLEW AHEAD.
LET'S KEEP THIS FRIENDLY, ALL RIGHT?
YOU DON'T WANT TO GO TO WAR WITH THE JUSTICE LEAGUE.
Geo-Force
YEAH... FRIENDLY.

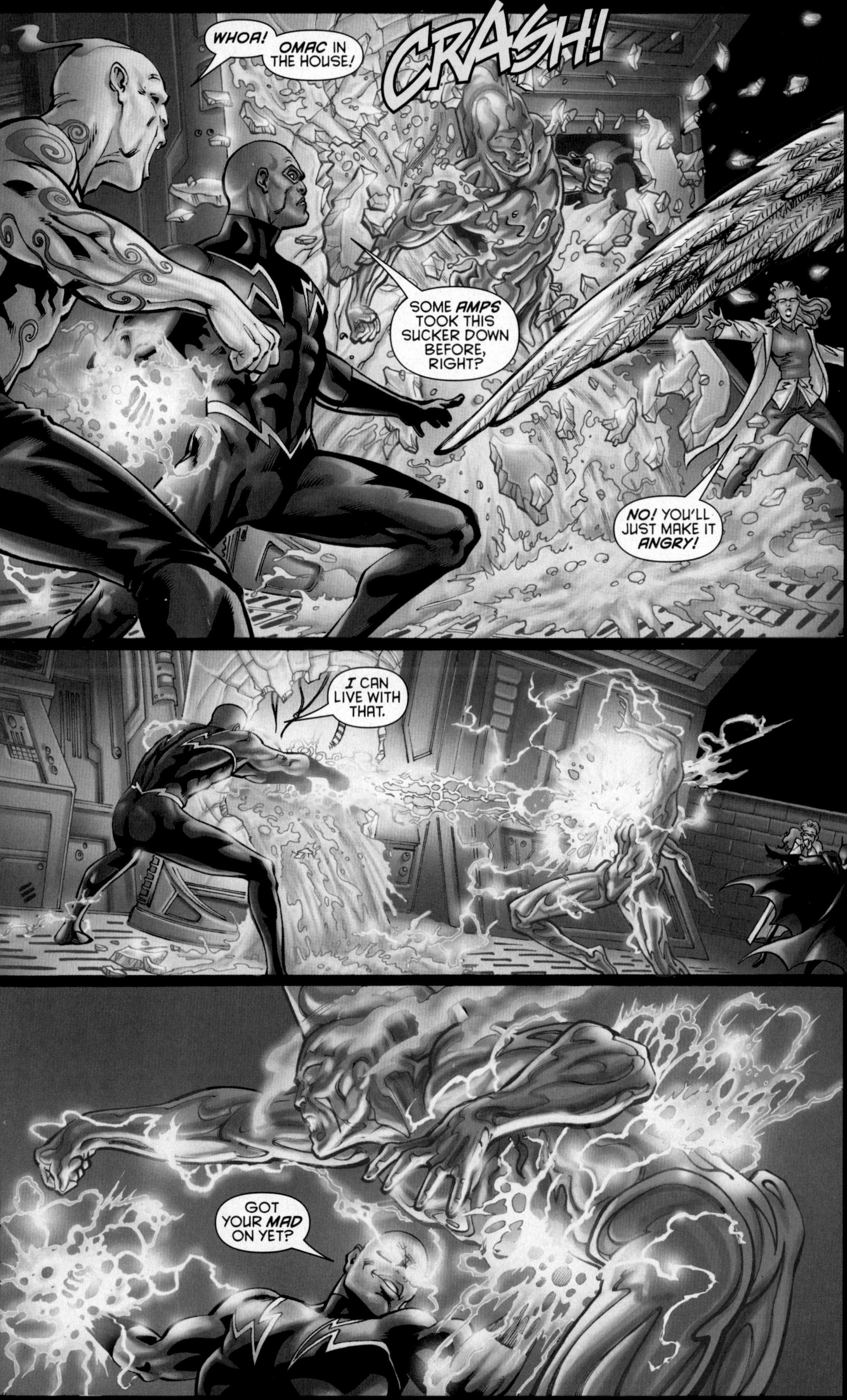
WHOA! OMAC IN THE HOUSE!
CRASH!
SOME AMPS TOOK THIS SUCKER DOWN BEFORE, RIGHT?
NO! YOU'LL JUST MAKE IT ANGRY!
I CAN LIVE WITH THAT.
GOT YOUR MAD ON YET?

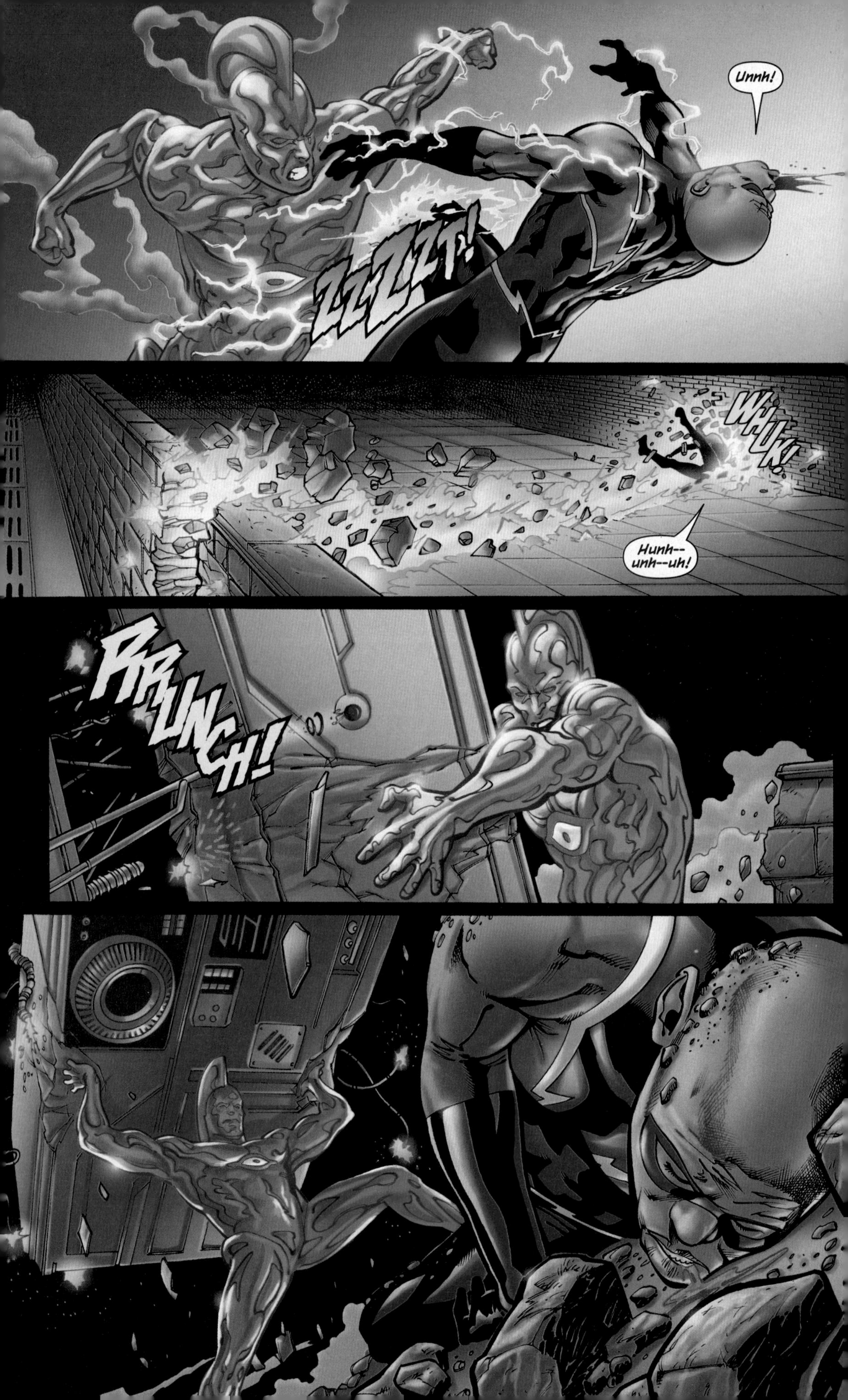
Unnh!
ZZ-ZZZT!
WHUK!
Hunh--
unh--uh!
RRUNCH!

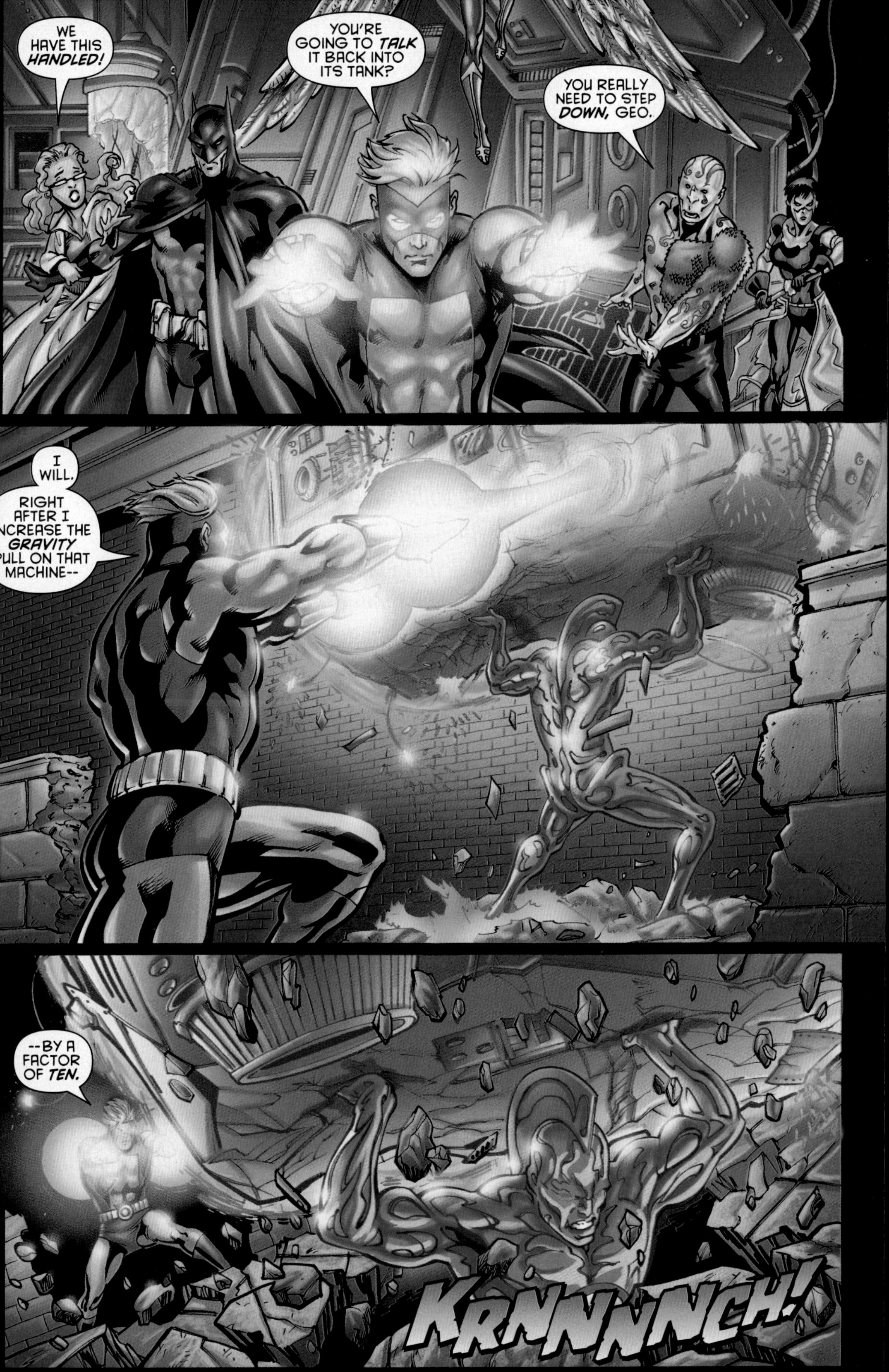
WE HAVE THIS HANDLED!
YOU'RE GOING TO TALK IT BACK INTO ITS TANK?
YOU REALLY NEED TO STEP DOWN, GEO.
I WILL.
RIGHT AFTER I INCREASE THE GRAVITY PULL ON THAT MACHINE--
--BY A FACTOR OF TEN.
KRNNNNCH!

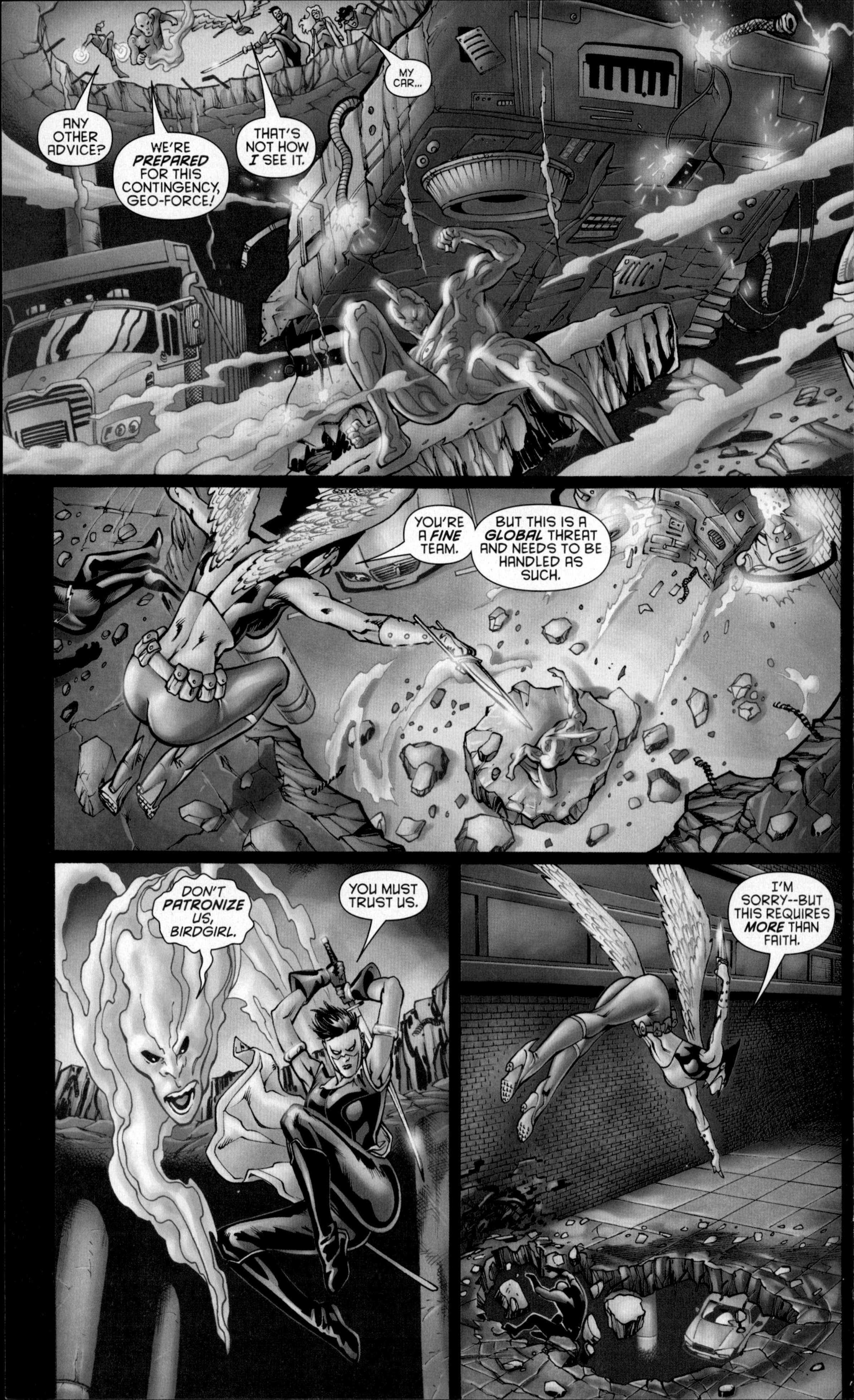
ANY OTHER ADVICE?
WE'RE PREPARED FOR THIS CONTINGENCY, GEO-FORCE!
THAT'S NOT HOW I SEE IT.
MY CAR...
YOU'RE A FINE TEAM.
BUT THIS IS A GLOBAL THREAT AND NEEDS TO BE HANDLED AS SUCH.
DON'T PATRONIZE US, BIRDGIRL.
YOU MUST TRUST US.
I'M SORRY--BUT THIS REQUIRES MORE THAN FAITH.

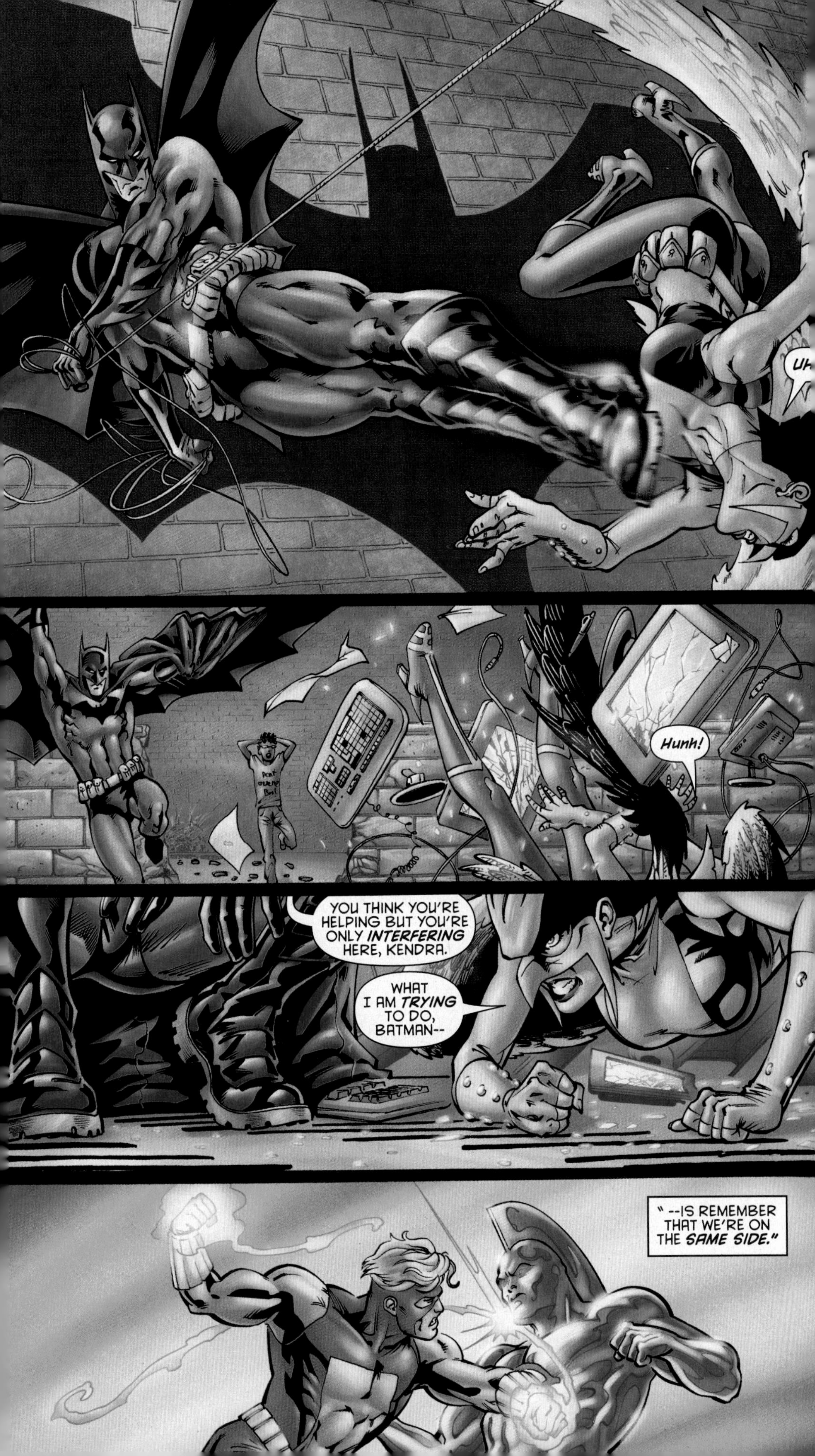
UH
Hunh!
YOU THINK YOU'RE HELPING BUT YOU'RE ONLY *INTERFERING* HERE, KENDRA.
WHAT I AM *TRYING* TO DO, BATMAN--
"--IS REMEMBER THAT WE'RE ON THE *SAME SIDE*."

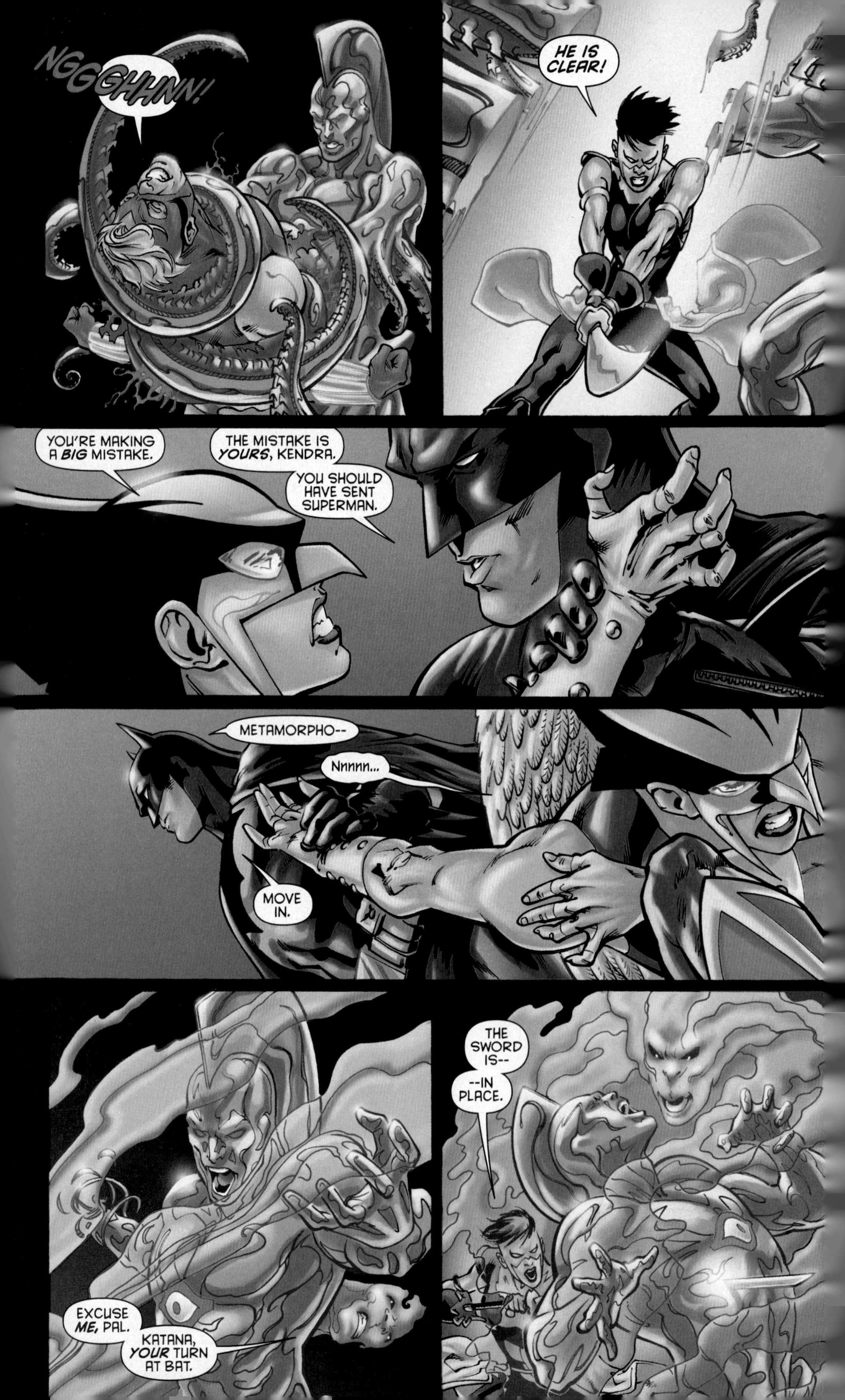
NGGGHHNN!
HE IS CLEAR!
YOU'RE MAKING A BIG MISTAKE.
THE MISTAKE IS YOURS, KENDRA.
YOU SHOULD HAVE SENT SUPERMAN.
METAMORPHO--
Nnnnn...
MOVE IN.
EXCUSE ME, PAL.
KATANA, YOUR TURN AT BAT.
THE SWORD IS--
--IN PLACE.

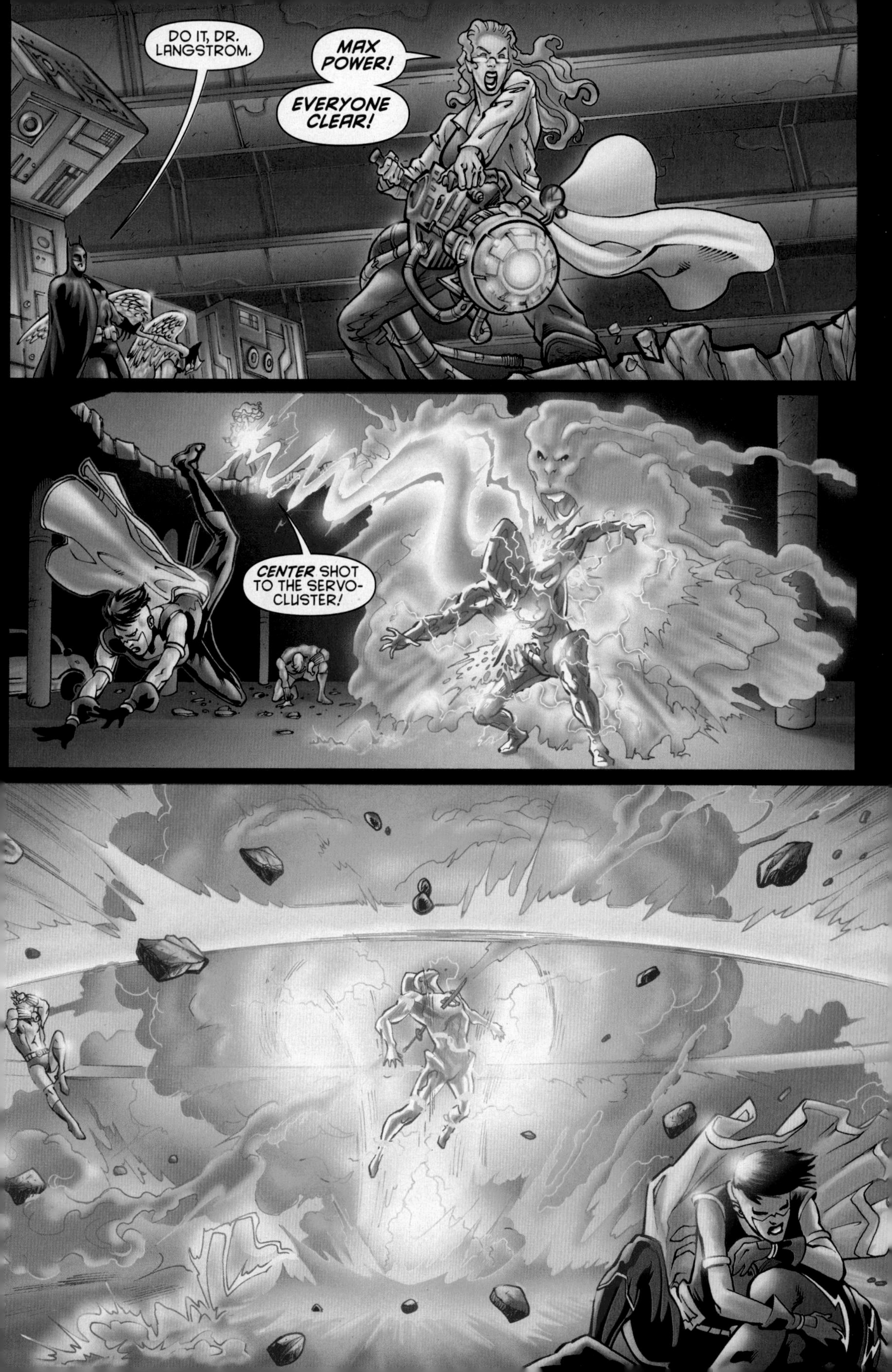
DO IT, DR. LANGSTROM.
MAX POWER!
EVERYONE CLEAR!
CENTER SHOT TO THE SERVO-CLUSTER!

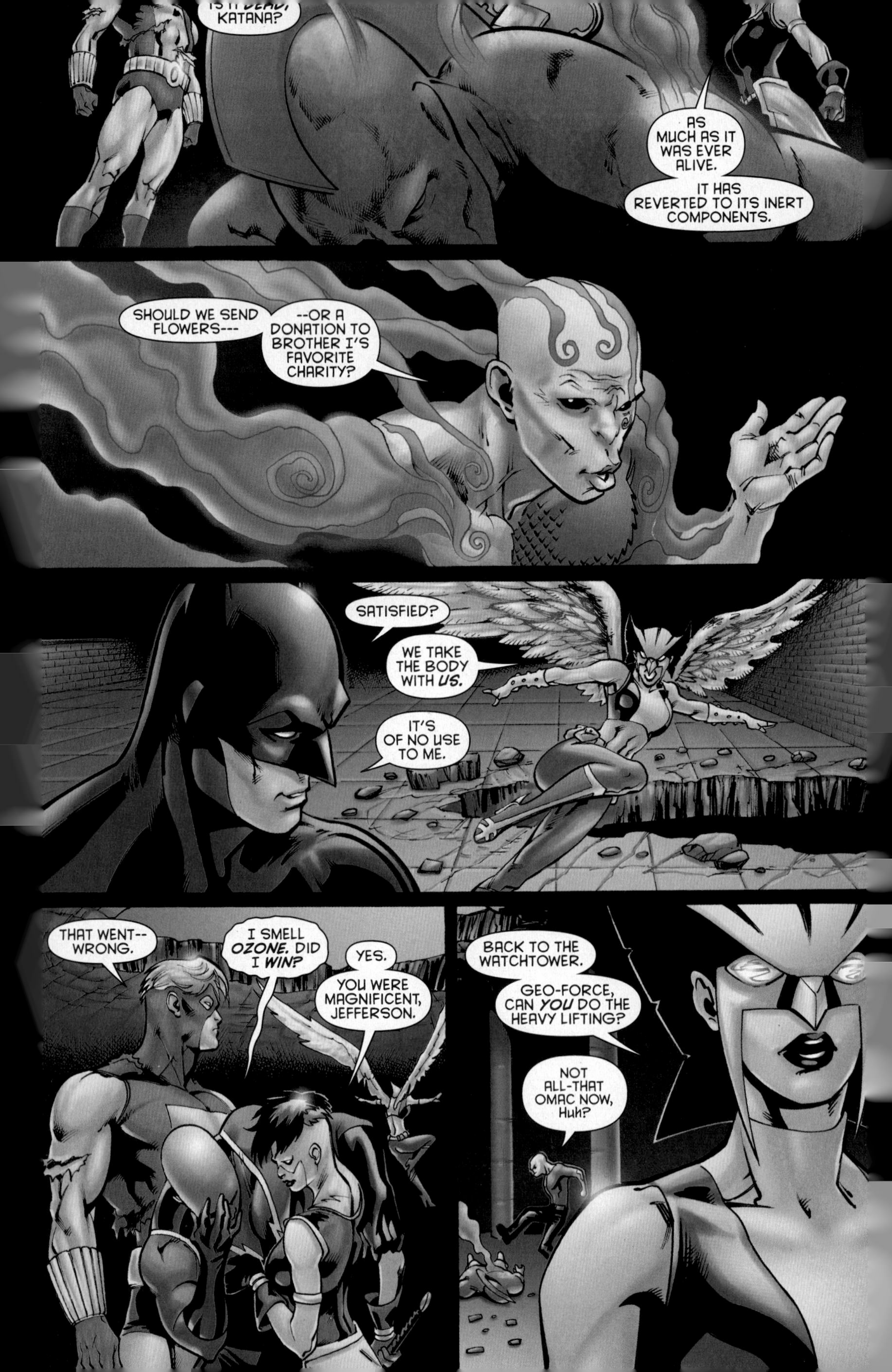
KATANA?
AS MUCH AS IT WAS EVER ALIVE.
IT HAS REVERTED TO ITS INERT COMPONENTS.
SHOULD WE SEND FLOWERS---
--OR A DONATION TO BROTHER I'S FAVORITE CHARITY?
SATISFIED?
WE TAKE THE BODY WITH *US*.
IT'S OF NO USE TO ME.
THAT WENT-- WRONG.
I SMELL *OZONE*. DID I *WIN?*
YES.
YOU WERE MAGNIFICENT, JEFFERSON.
BACK TO THE WATCHTOWER.
GEO-FORCE, CAN *YOU* DO THE HEAVY LIFTING?
NOT ALL-THAT OMAC NOW, Huh?

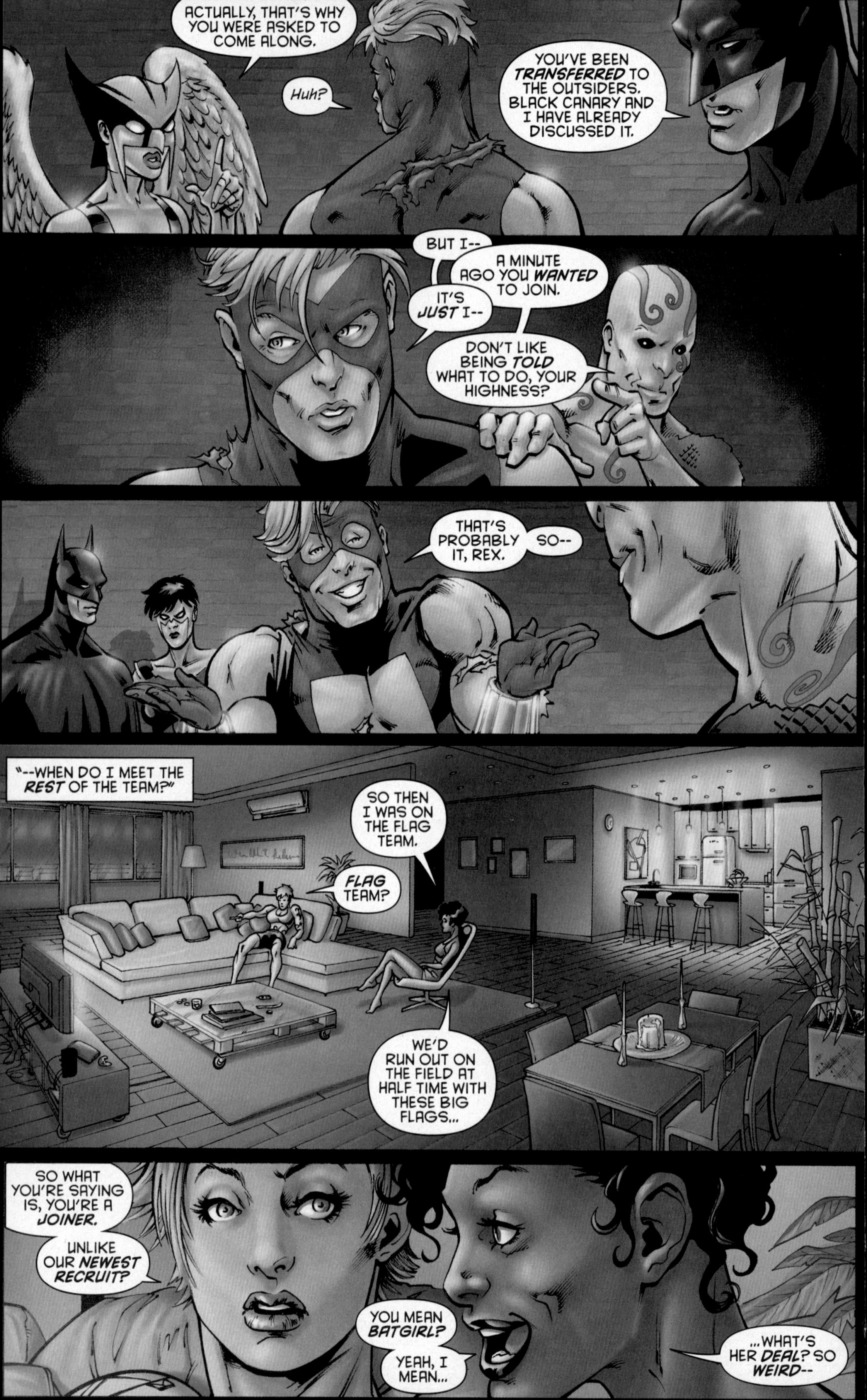
ACTUALLY, THAT'S WHY YOU WERE ASKED TO COME ALONG.
Huh?
YOU'VE BEEN *TRANSFERRED* TO THE OUTSIDERS. BLACK CANARY AND I HAVE ALREADY DISCUSSED IT.
BUT I--
A MINUTE AGO YOU *WANTED* TO JOIN.
IT'S *JUST* I--
DON'T LIKE BEING *TOLD* WHAT TO DO, YOUR HIGHNESS?
THAT'S PROBABLY IT, REX.
SO--
"--WHEN DO I MEET THE *REST* OF THE TEAM?"
SO THEN I WAS ON THE FLAG TEAM.
FLAG TEAM?
WE'D RUN OUT ON THE FIELD AT HALF TIME WITH THESE BIG FLAGS...
SO WHAT YOU'RE SAYING IS, YOU'RE A *JOINER*.
UNLIKE OUR *NEWEST RECRUIT*?
YOU MEAN *BATGIRL*?
YEAH, I MEAN...
...WHAT'S HER *DEAL*? SO *WEIRD*--

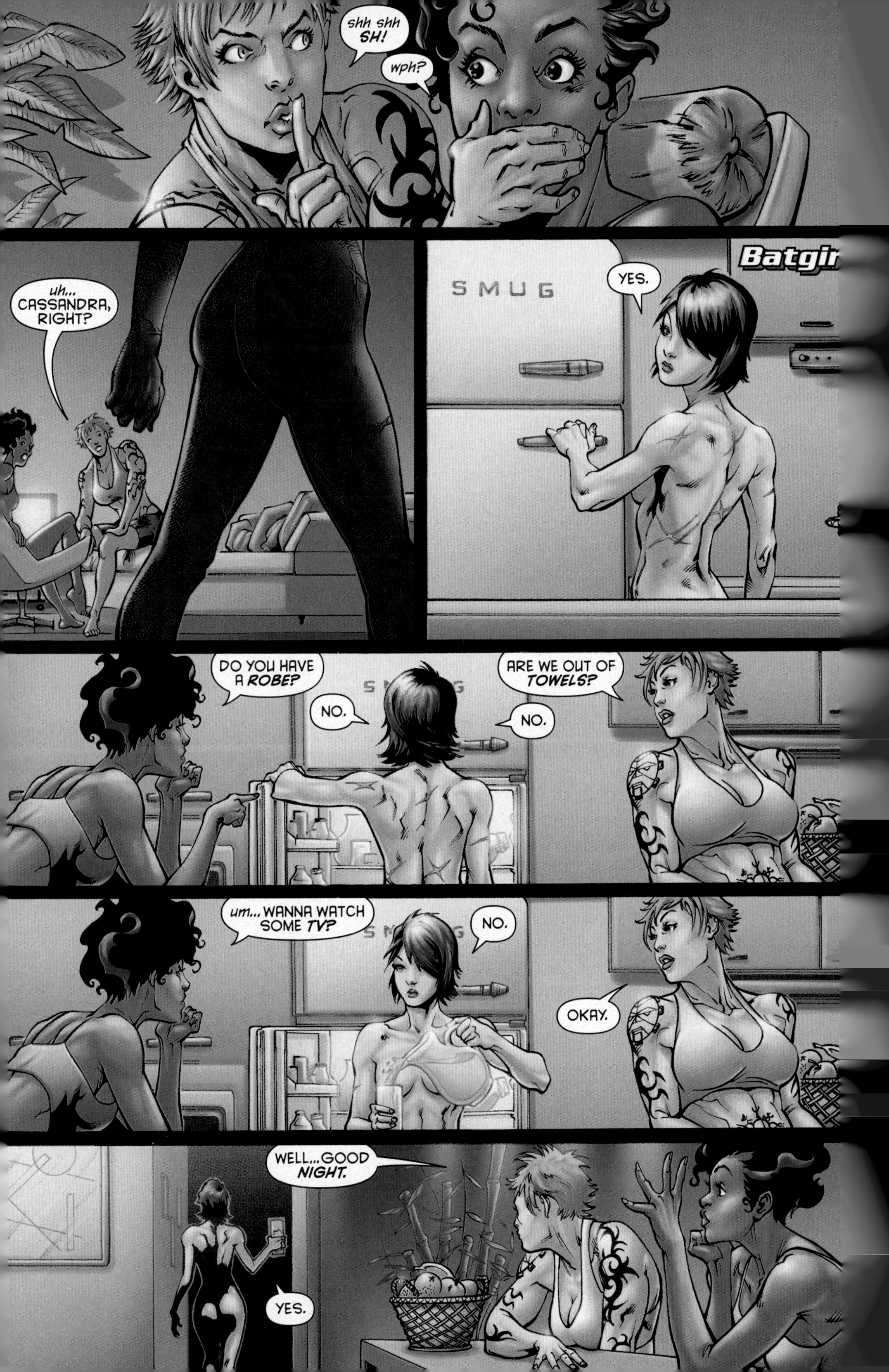

shh shh SH!
wph?
uh... CASSANDRA, RIGHT?
Batgir
YES.
DO YOU HAVE A ROBE?
NO.
ARE WE OUT OF TOWELS?
NO.
um... WANNA WATCH SOME TV?
NO.
OKAY.
WELL... GOOD NIGHT.
YES.

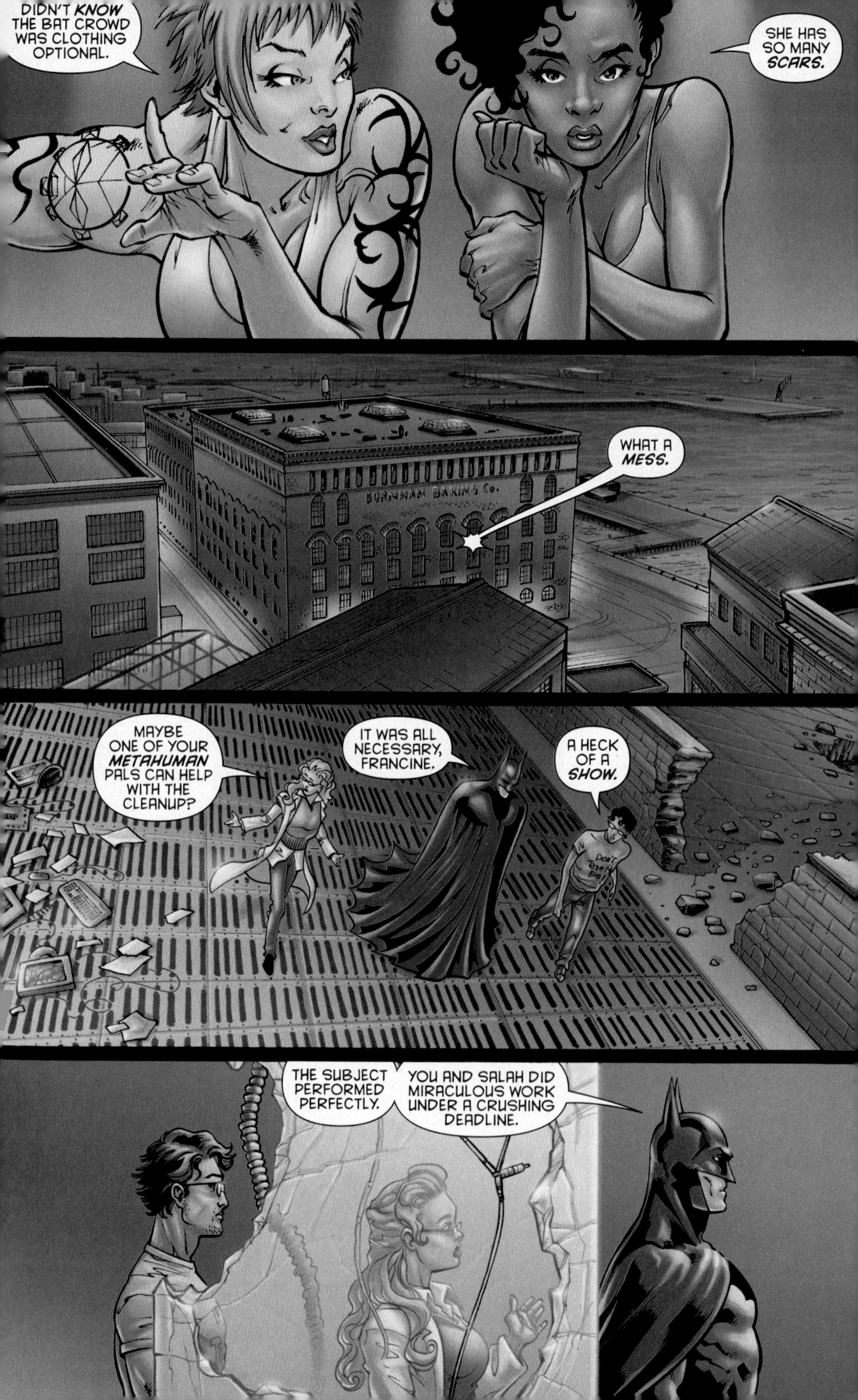

DIDN'T KNOW THE BAT CROWD WAS CLOTHING OPTIONAL.
SHE HAS SO MANY SCARS.
WHAT A MESS.
BURNHAM BAKING Co.
MAYBE ONE OF YOUR METAHUMAN PALS CAN HELP WITH THE CLEANUP?
IT WAS ALL NECESSARY, FRANCINE.
A HECK OF A SHOW.
THE SUBJECT PERFORMED PERFECTLY.
YOU AND SALAH DID MIRACULOUS WORK UNDER A CRUSHING DEADLINE.

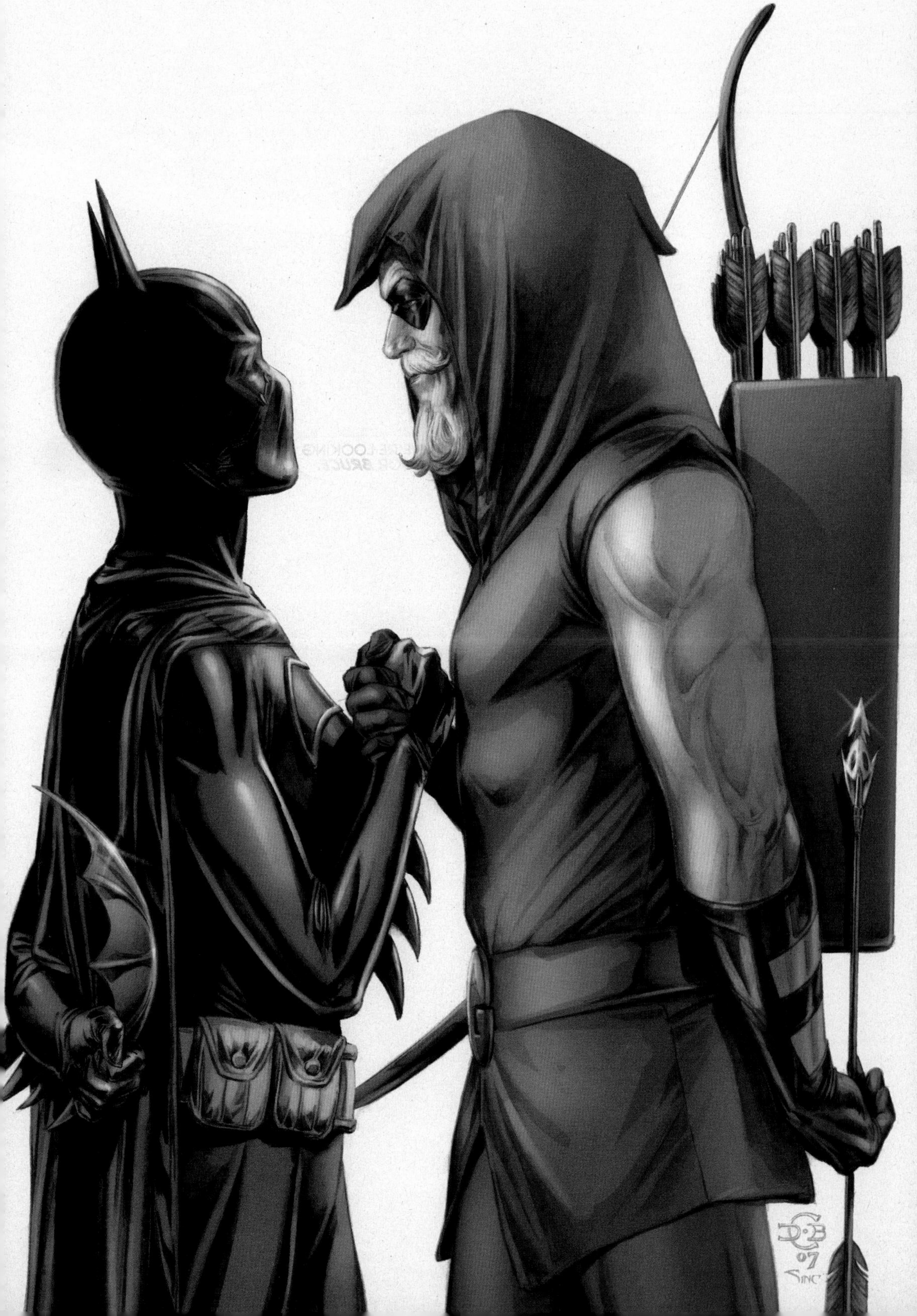

part FOUR

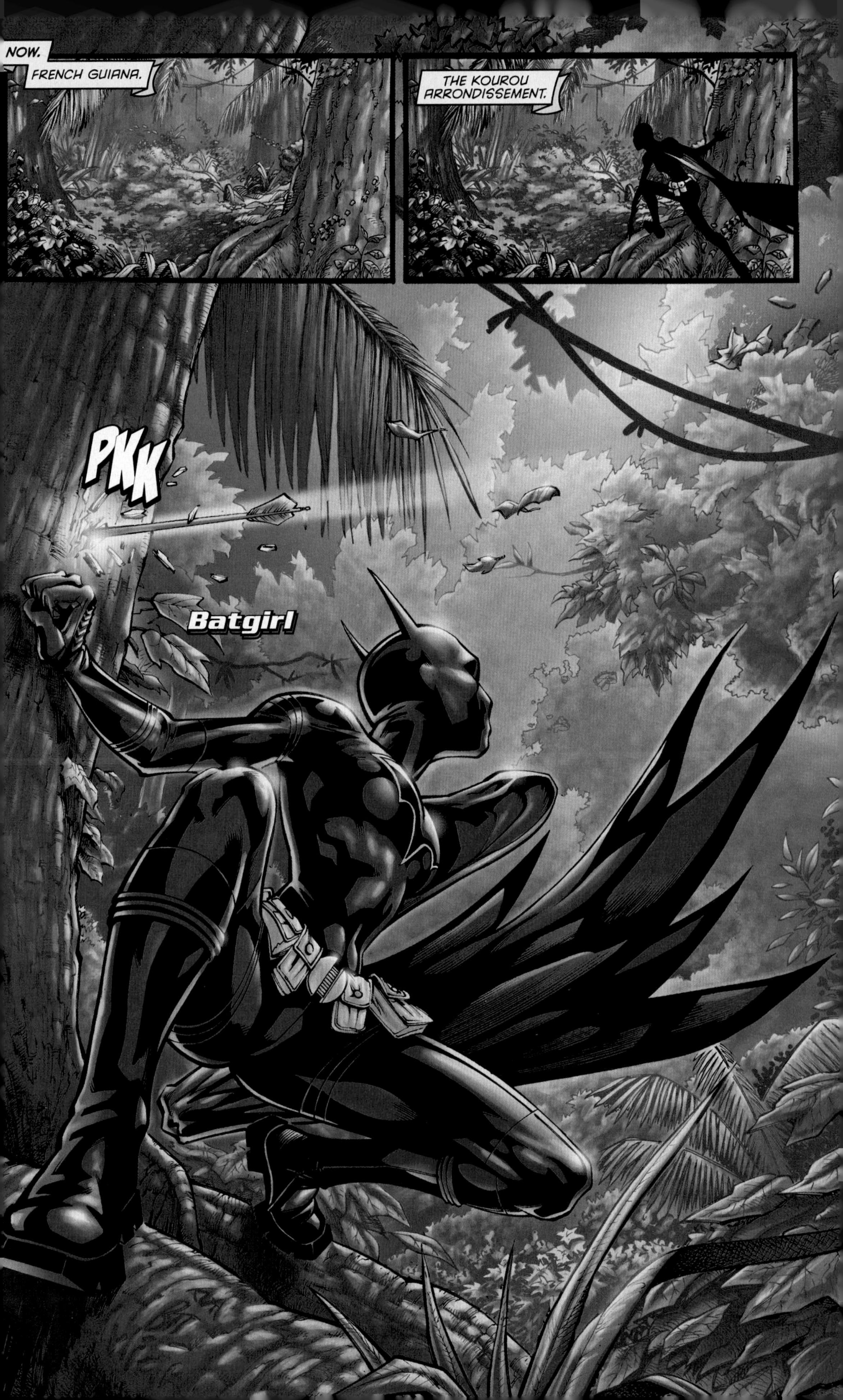
NOW.
FRENCH GUIANA.
THE KOUROU ARRONDISSEMENT.
PKK
Batgirl

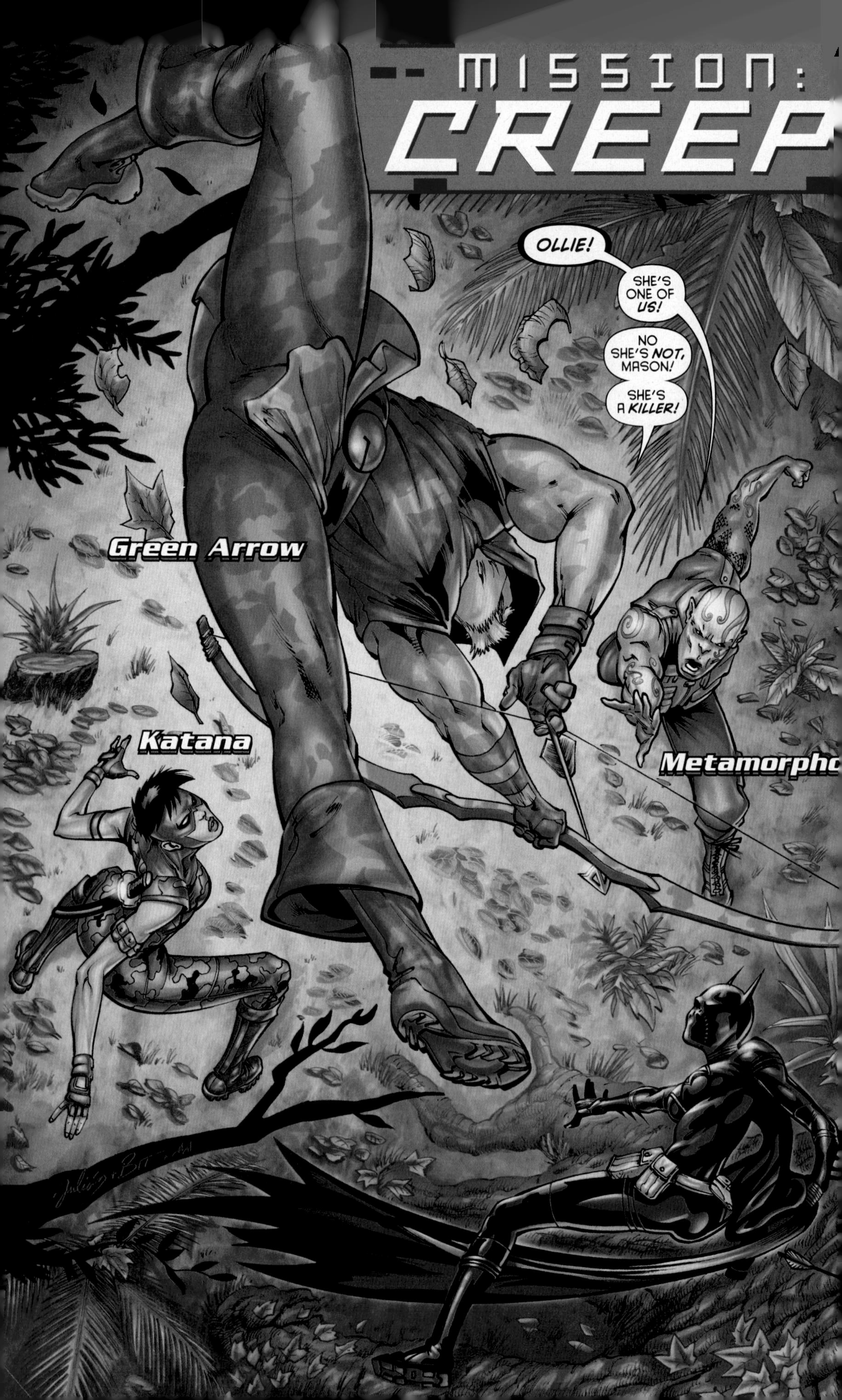
MISSION:
CREEP
OLLIE!
SHE'S ONE OF US!
NO SHE'S NOT, MASON!
SHE'S A KILLER!
Green Arrow
Katana
Metamorpho

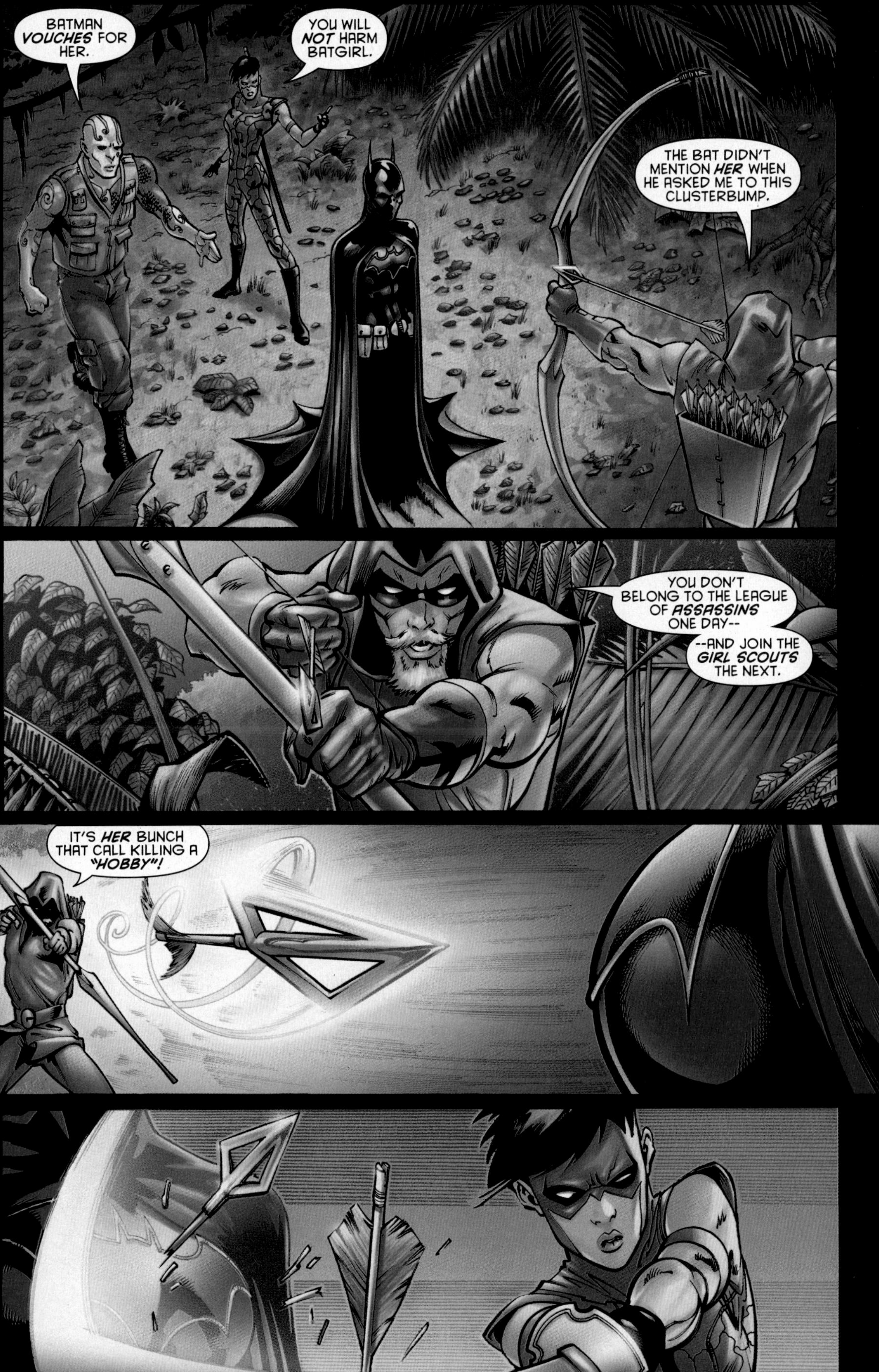
BATMAN VOUCHES FOR HER.
YOU WILL NOT HARM BATGIRL.
THE BAT DIDN'T MENTION HER WHEN HE ASKED ME TO THIS CLUSTERBUMP.
YOU DON'T BELONG TO THE LEAGUE OF ASSASSINS ONE DAY--
--AND JOIN THE GIRL SCOUTS THE NEXT.
IT'S HER BUNCH THAT CALL KILLING A "HOBBY"!

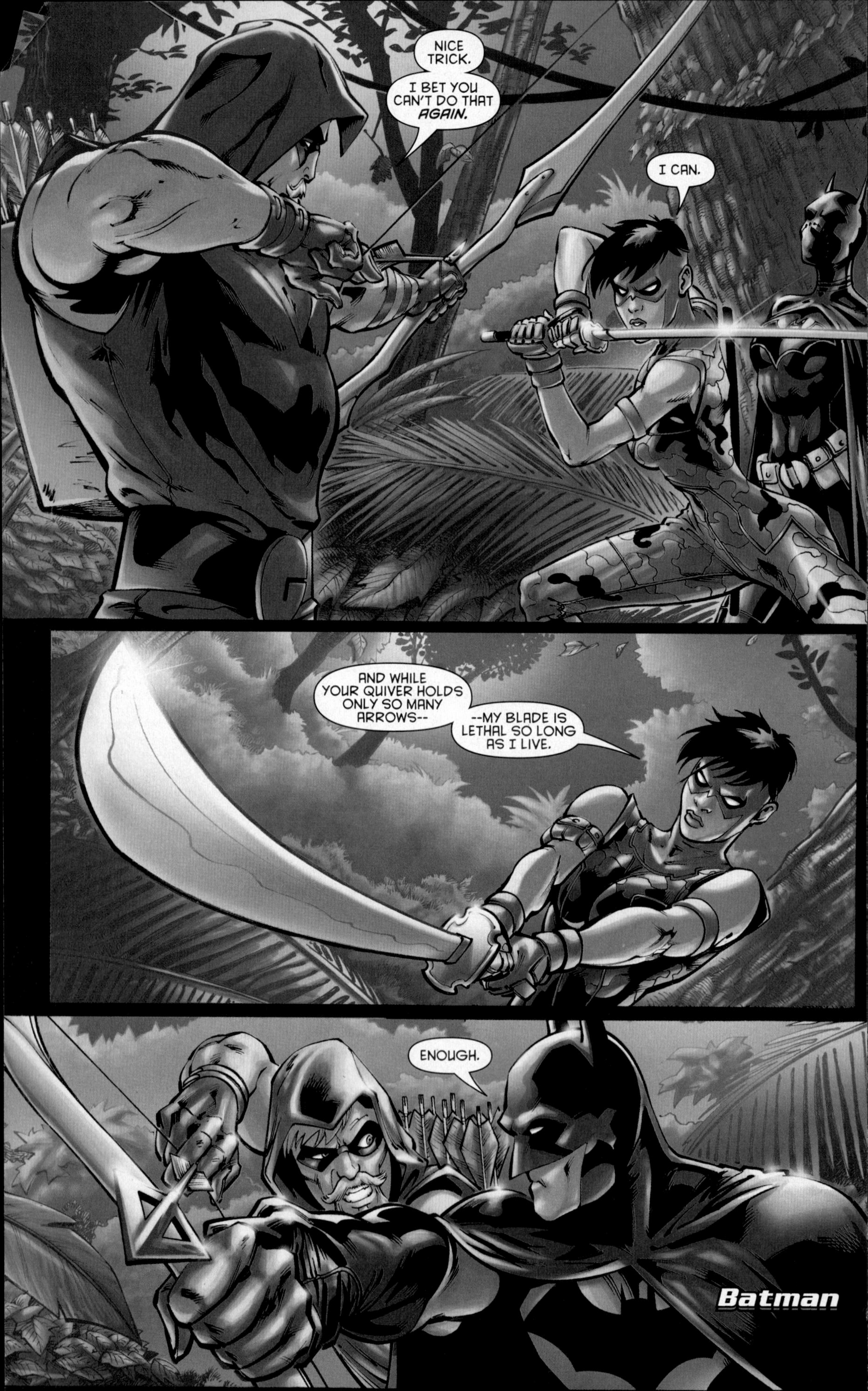
NICE TRICK.
I BET YOU CAN'T DO THAT *AGAIN.*
I CAN.
AND WHILE YOUR QUIVER HOLDS ONLY SO MANY ARROWS--
--MY BLADE IS LETHAL SO LONG AS I LIVE.
ENOUGH.
Batman

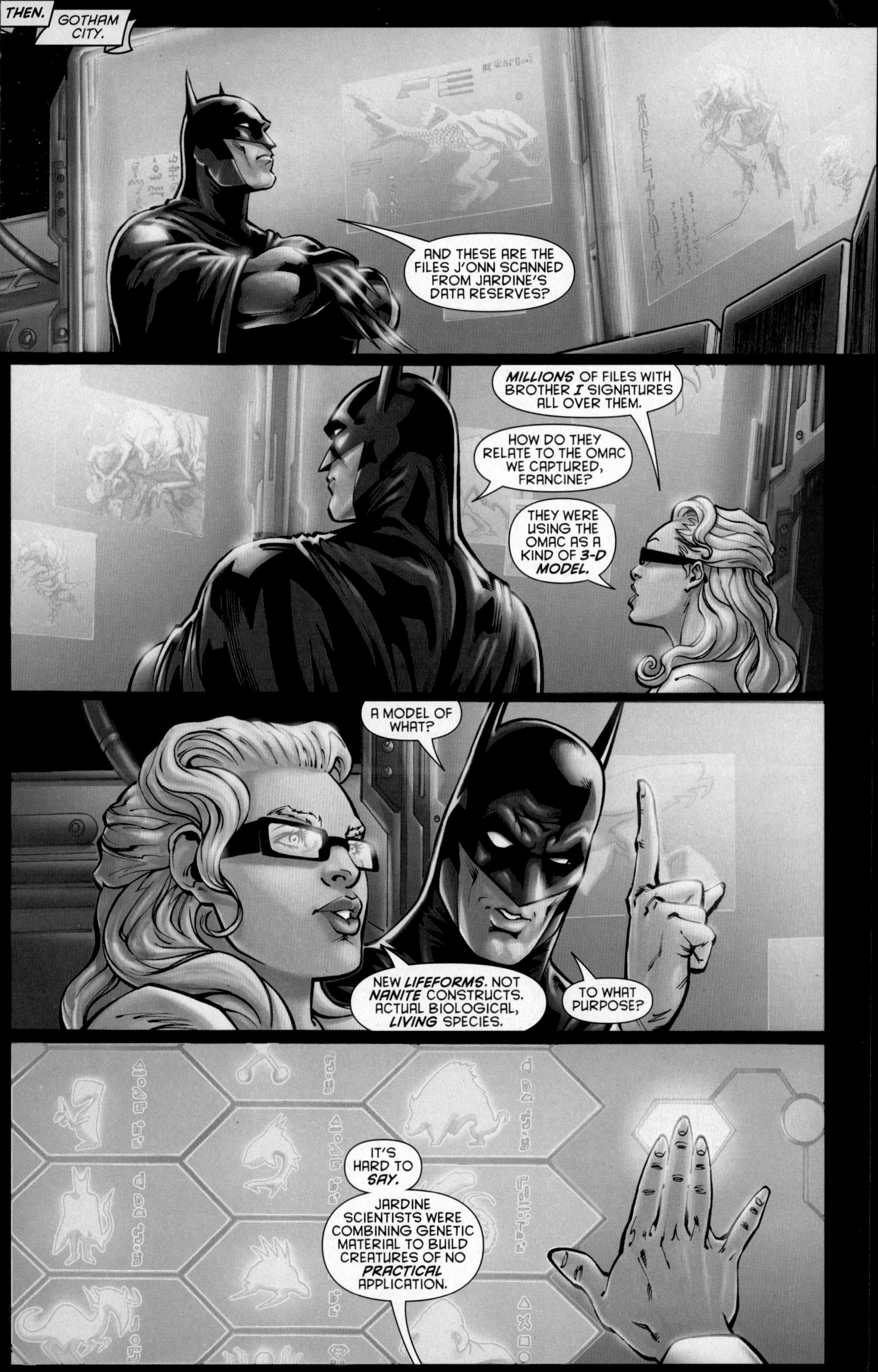
THEN.
GOTHAM CITY.
AND THESE ARE THE FILES J'ONN SCANNED FROM JARDINE'S DATA RESERVES?
MILLIONS OF FILES WITH BROTHER I SIGNATURES ALL OVER THEM.
HOW DO THEY RELATE TO THE OMAC WE CAPTURED, FRANCINE?
THEY WERE USING THE OMAC AS A KIND OF 3-D MODEL.
A MODEL OF WHAT?
NEW LIFEFORMS. NOT NANITE CONSTRUCTS. ACTUAL BIOLOGICAL, LIVING SPECIES.
TO WHAT PURPOSE?
IT'S HARD TO SAY.
JARDINE SCIENTISTS WERE COMBINING GENETIC MATERIAL TO BUILD CREATURES OF NO PRACTICAL APPLICATION.

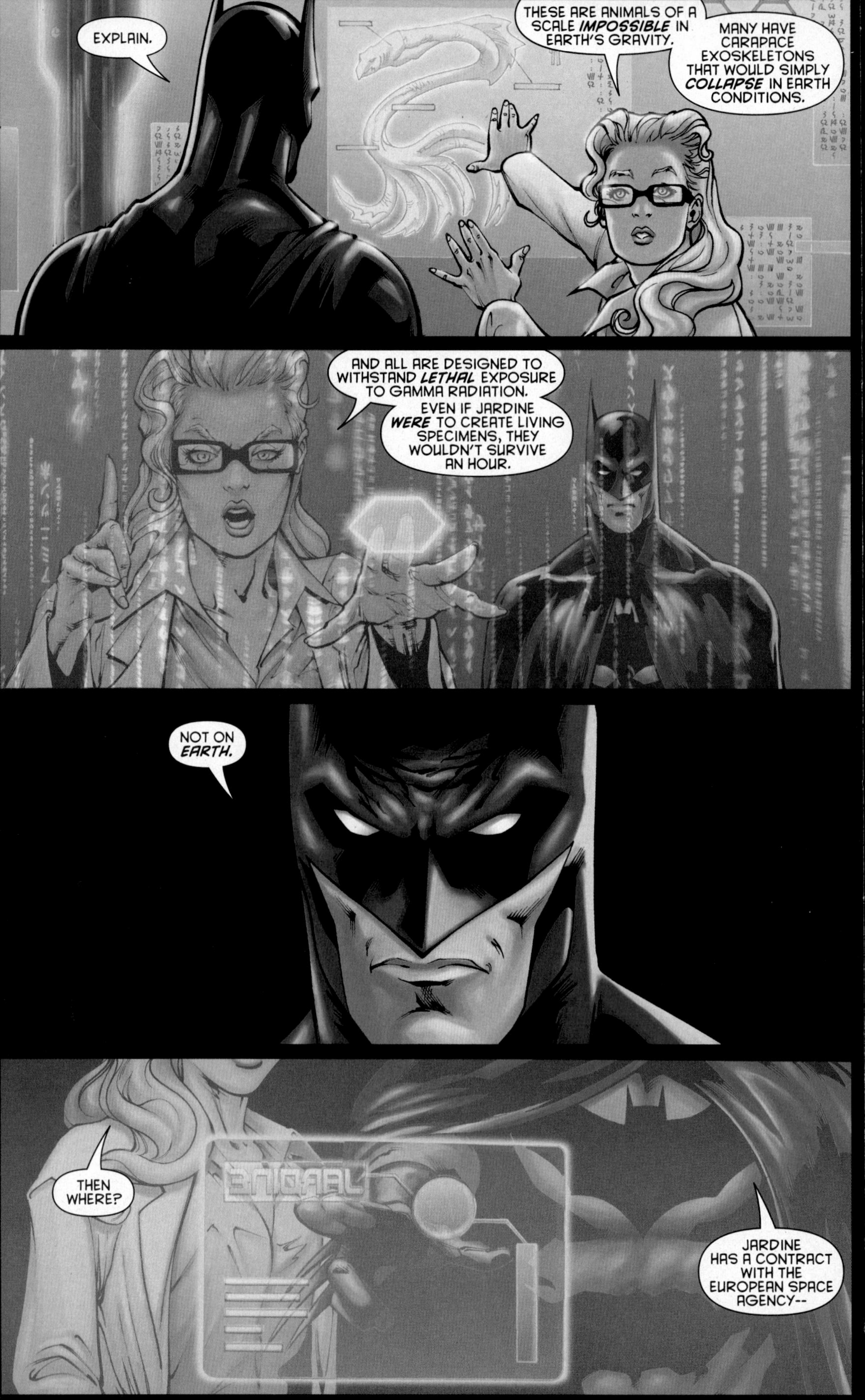
EXPLAIN.
THESE ARE ANIMALS OF A SCALE IMPOSSIBLE IN EARTH'S GRAVITY.
MANY HAVE CARAPACE EXOSKELETONS THAT WOULD SIMPLY COLLAPSE IN EARTH CONDITIONS.
AND ALL ARE DESIGNED TO WITHSTAND LETHAL EXPOSURE TO GAMMA RADIATION.
EVEN IF JARDINE WERE TO CREATE LIVING SPECIMENS, THEY WOULDN'T SURVIVE AN HOUR.
NOT ON EARTH.
THEN WHERE?
JARDINE HAS A CONTRACT WITH THE EUROPEAN SPACE AGENCY--

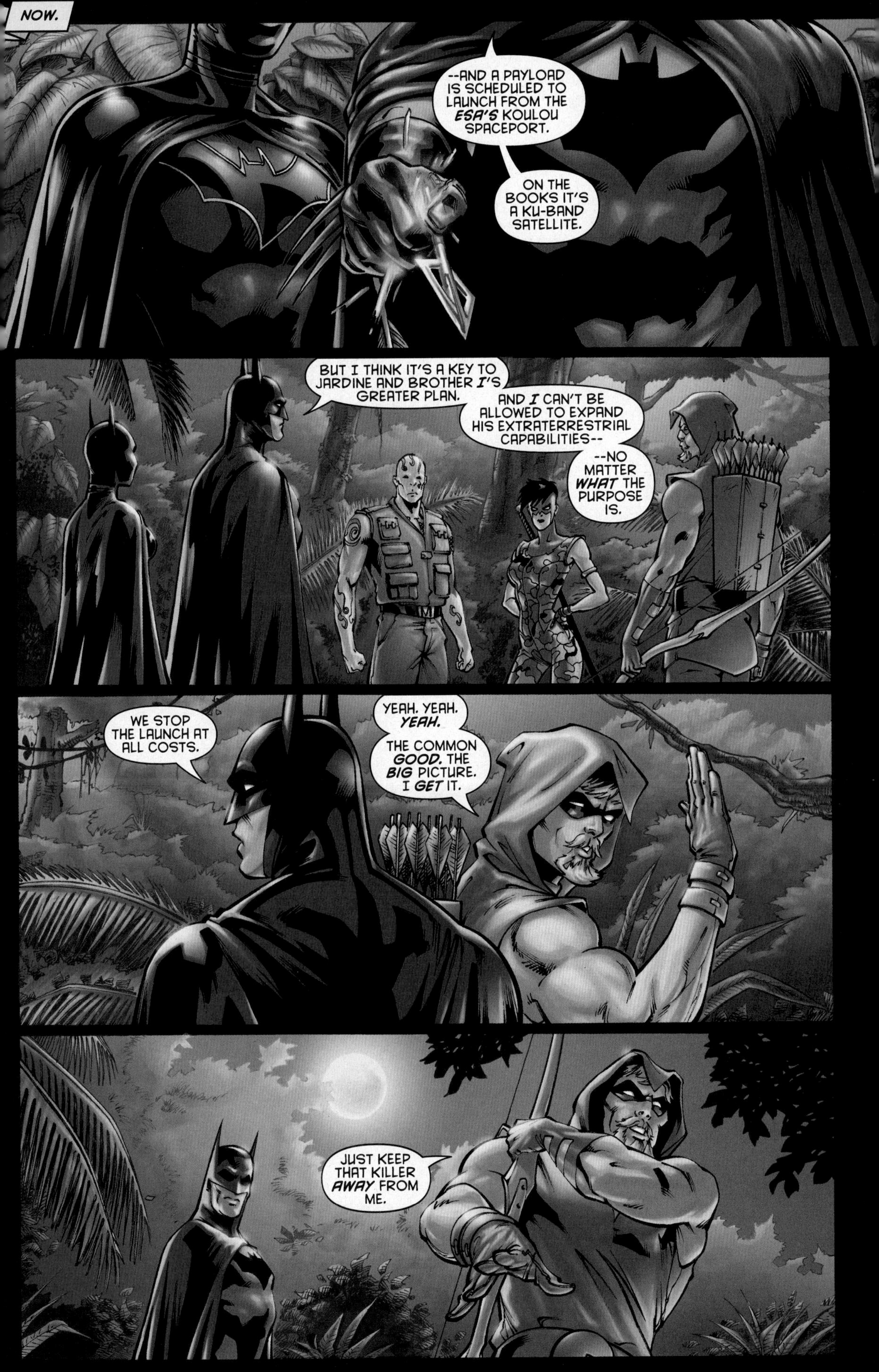
NOW.
--AND A PAYLOAD IS SCHEDULED TO LAUNCH FROM THE ESA'S KOULOU SPACEPORT.
ON THE BOOKS IT'S A KU-BAND SATELLITE.
BUT I THINK IT'S A KEY TO JARDINE AND BROTHER I'S GREATER PLAN.
AND I CAN'T BE ALLOWED TO EXPAND HIS EXTRATERRESTRIAL CAPABILITIES--
--NO MATTER WHAT THE PURPOSE IS.
WE STOP THE LAUNCH AT ALL COSTS.
YEAH. YEAH. YEAH.
THE COMMON GOOD. THE BIG PICTURE. I GET IT.
JUST KEEP THAT KILLER AWAY FROM ME.

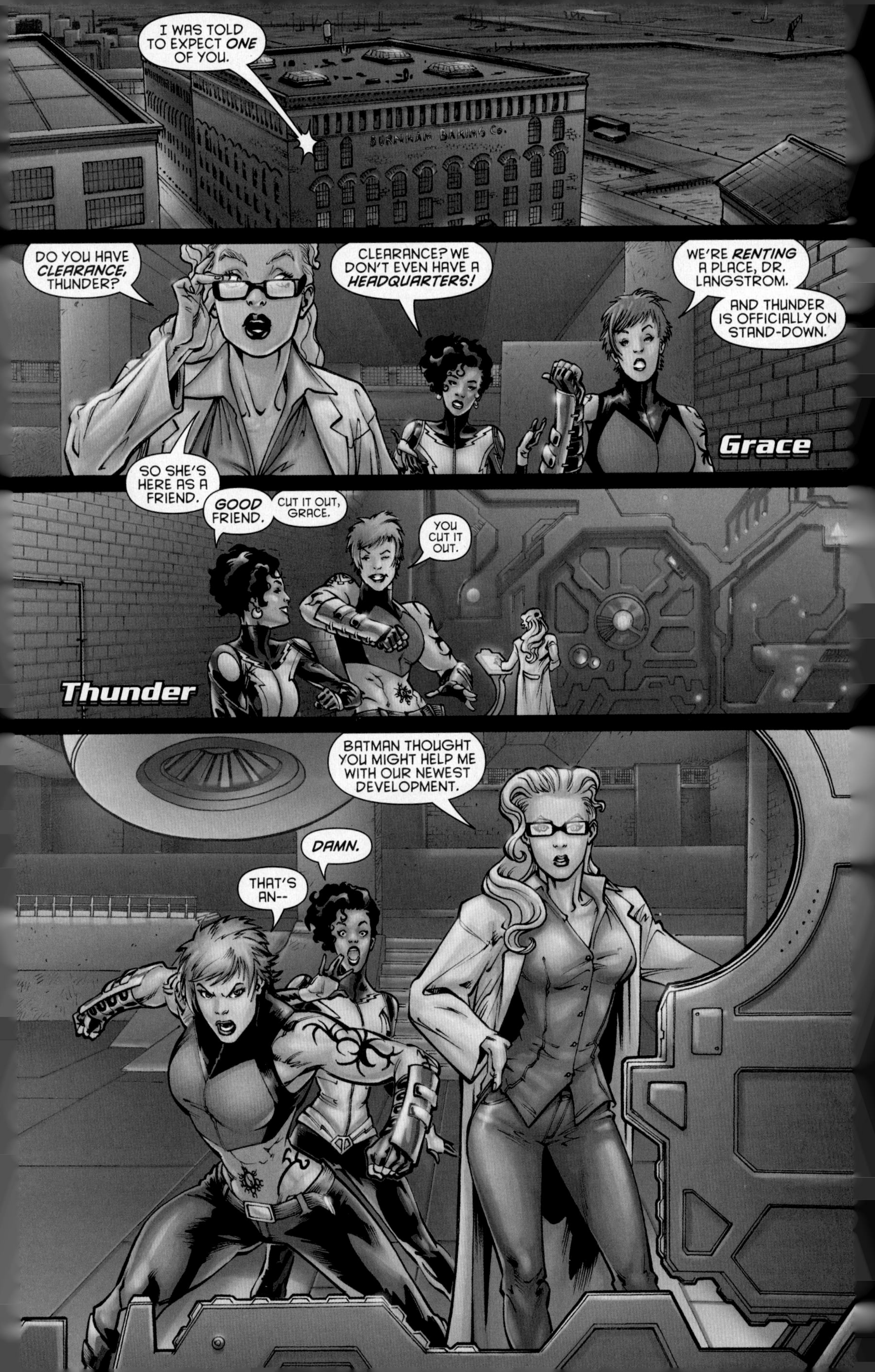
I WAS TOLD TO EXPECT *ONE* OF YOU.
BURNHAM BAKING Co.
DO YOU HAVE *CLEARANCE,* THUNDER?
CLEARANCE? WE DON'T EVEN HAVE A *HEADQUARTERS!*
WE'RE *RENTING* A PLACE, DR. LANGSTROM.
AND THUNDER IS OFFICIALLY ON STAND-DOWN.
Grace
SO SHE'S HERE AS A FRIEND.
GOOD FRIEND.
CUT IT OUT, GRACE.
YOU CUT IT OUT.
Thunder
BATMAN THOUGHT YOU MIGHT HELP ME WITH OUR NEWEST DEVELOPMENT.
DAMN.
THAT'S AN--

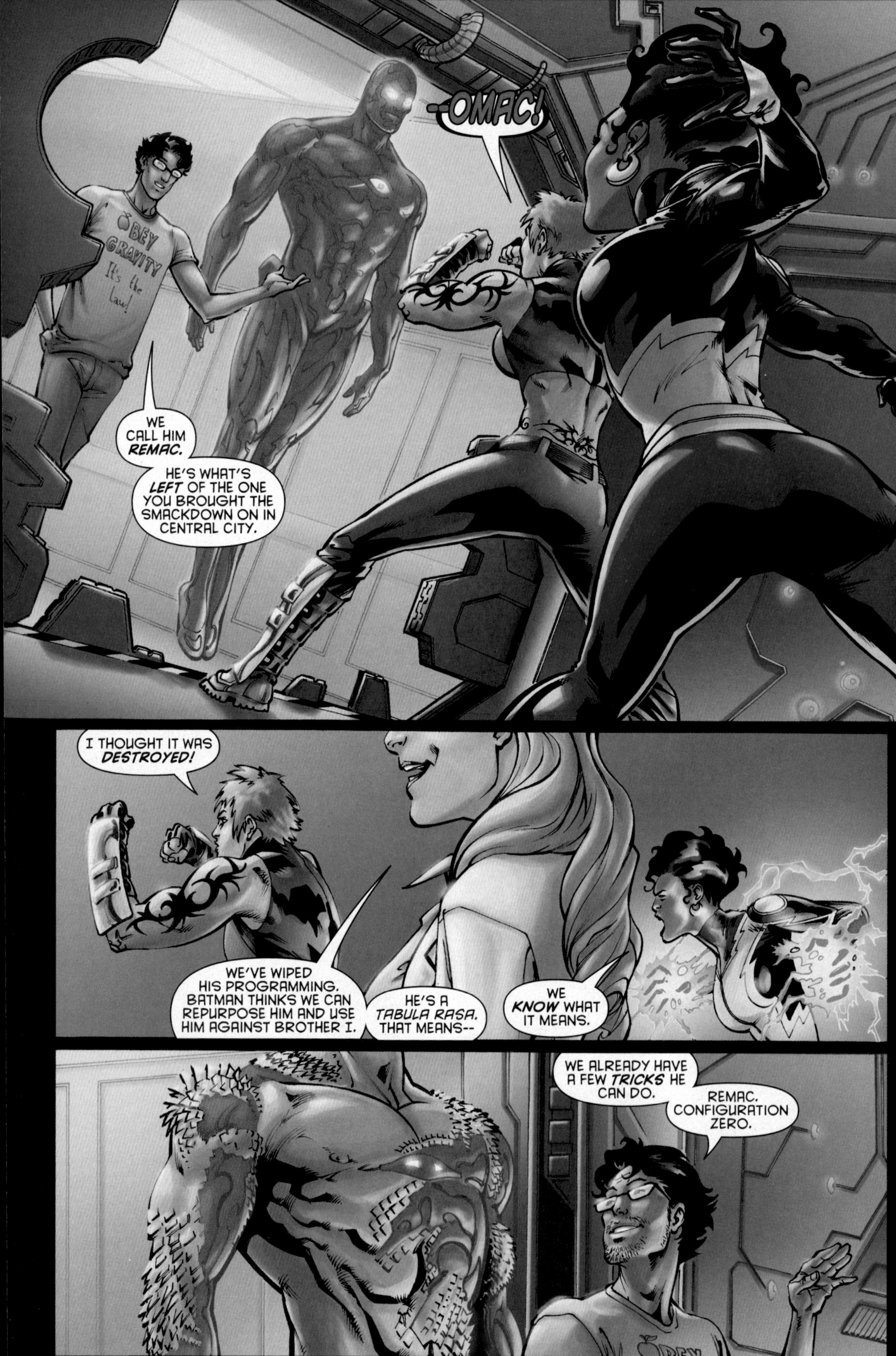

-OMAC!
OBEY GRAVITY It's the law!
WE CALL HIM *REMAC.*
HE'S WHAT'S *LEFT* OF THE ONE YOU BROUGHT THE SMACKDOWN ON IN CENTRAL CITY.
I THOUGHT IT WAS *DESTROYED!*
WE'VE WIPED HIS PROGRAMMING. BATMAN THINKS WE CAN REPURPOSE HIM AND USE HIM AGAINST BROTHER I.
HE'S A *TABULA RASA.* THAT MEANS--
WE *KNOW* WHAT IT MEANS.
WE ALREADY HAVE A FEW *TRICKS* HE CAN DO.
REMAC. CONFIGURATION ZERO.

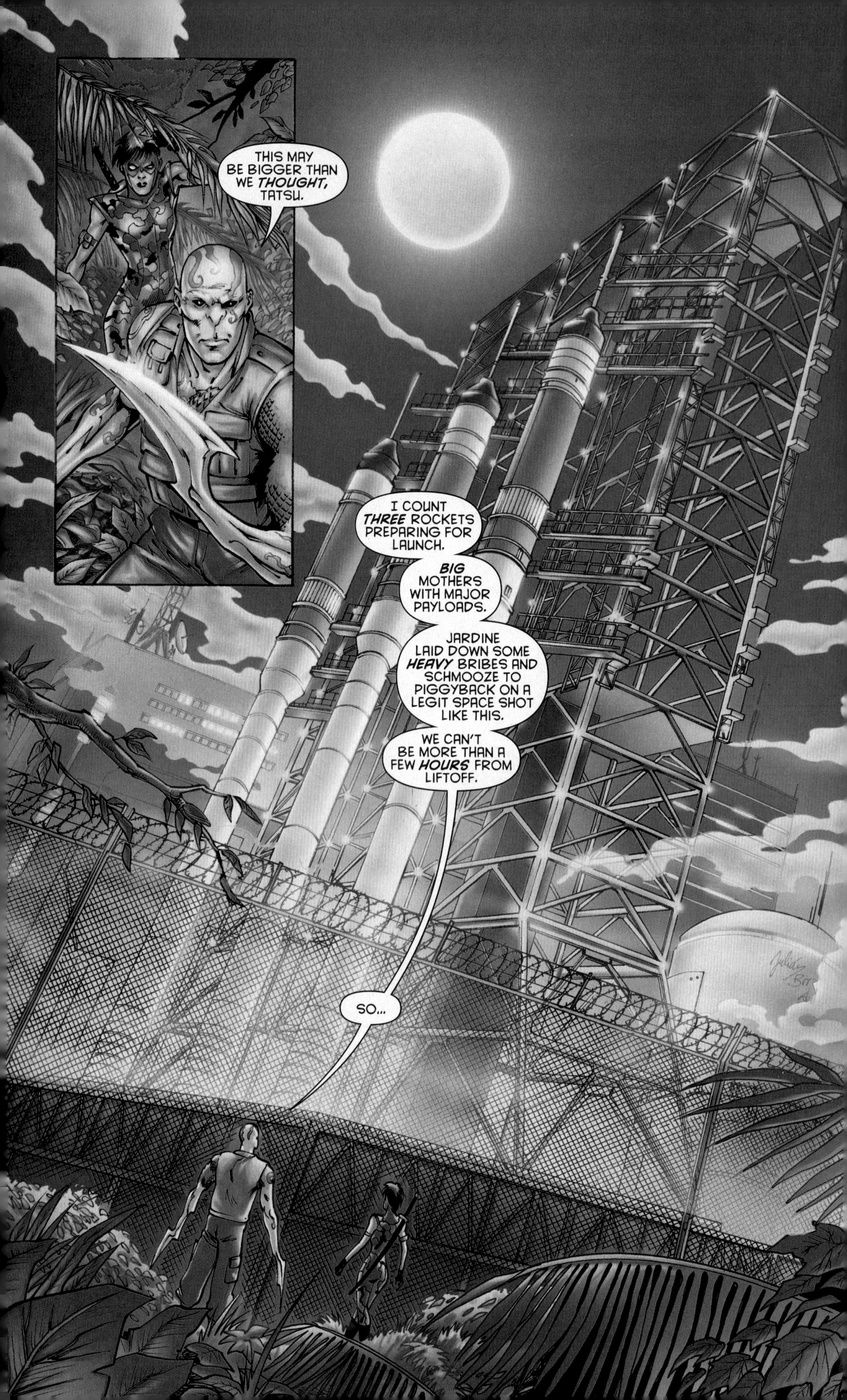
THIS MAY BE BIGGER THAN WE THOUGHT, TATSU.
I COUNT THREE ROCKETS PREPARING FOR LAUNCH.
BIG MOTHERS WITH MAJOR PAYLOADS.
JARDINE LAID DOWN SOME HEAVY BRIBES AND SCHMOOZE TO PIGGYBACK ON A LEGIT SPACE SHOT LIKE THIS.
WE CAN'T BE MORE THAN A FEW HOURS FROM LIFTOFF.
SO...

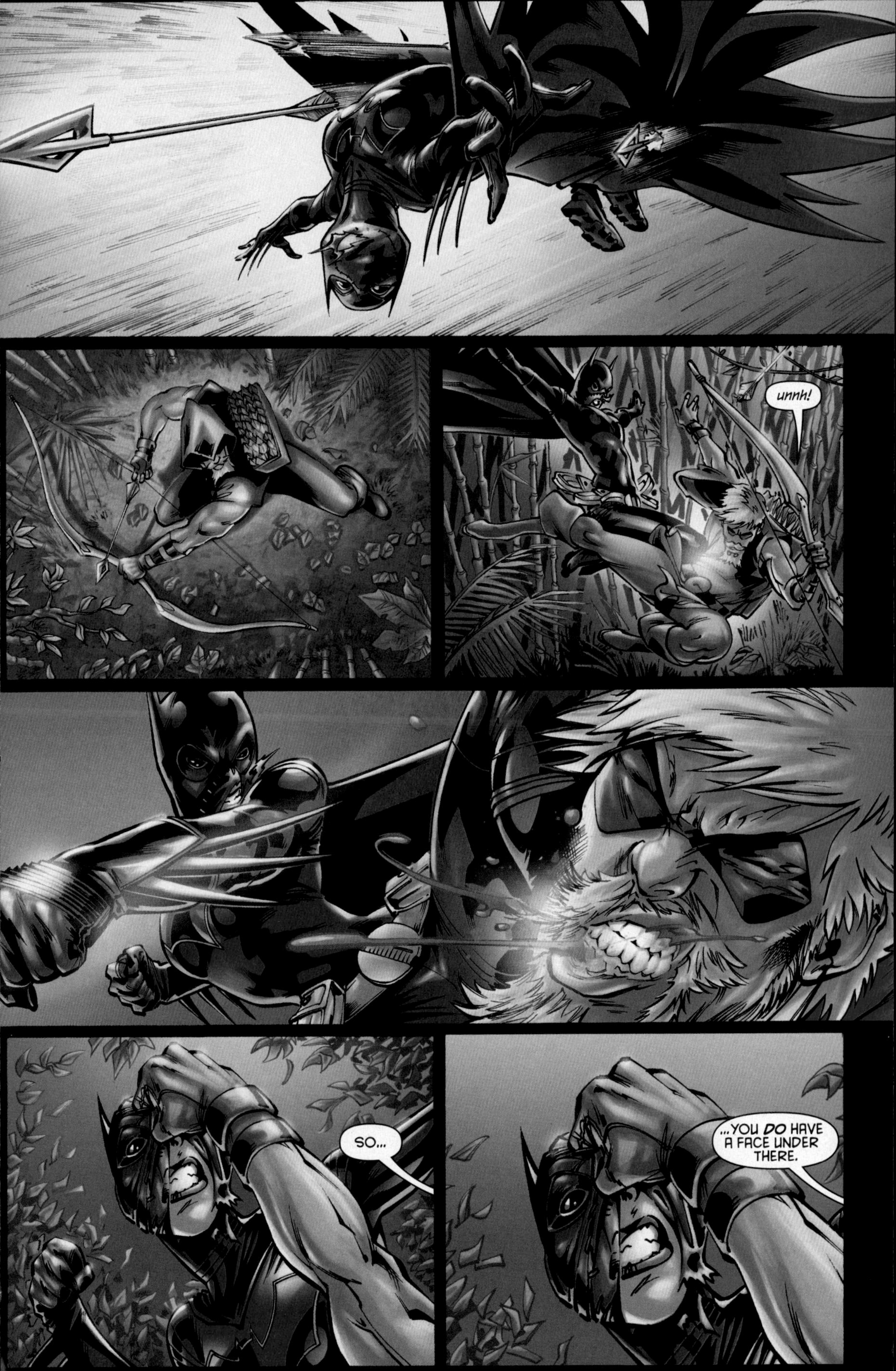
unnh!
SO...
...YOU DO HAVE A FACE UNDER THERE.

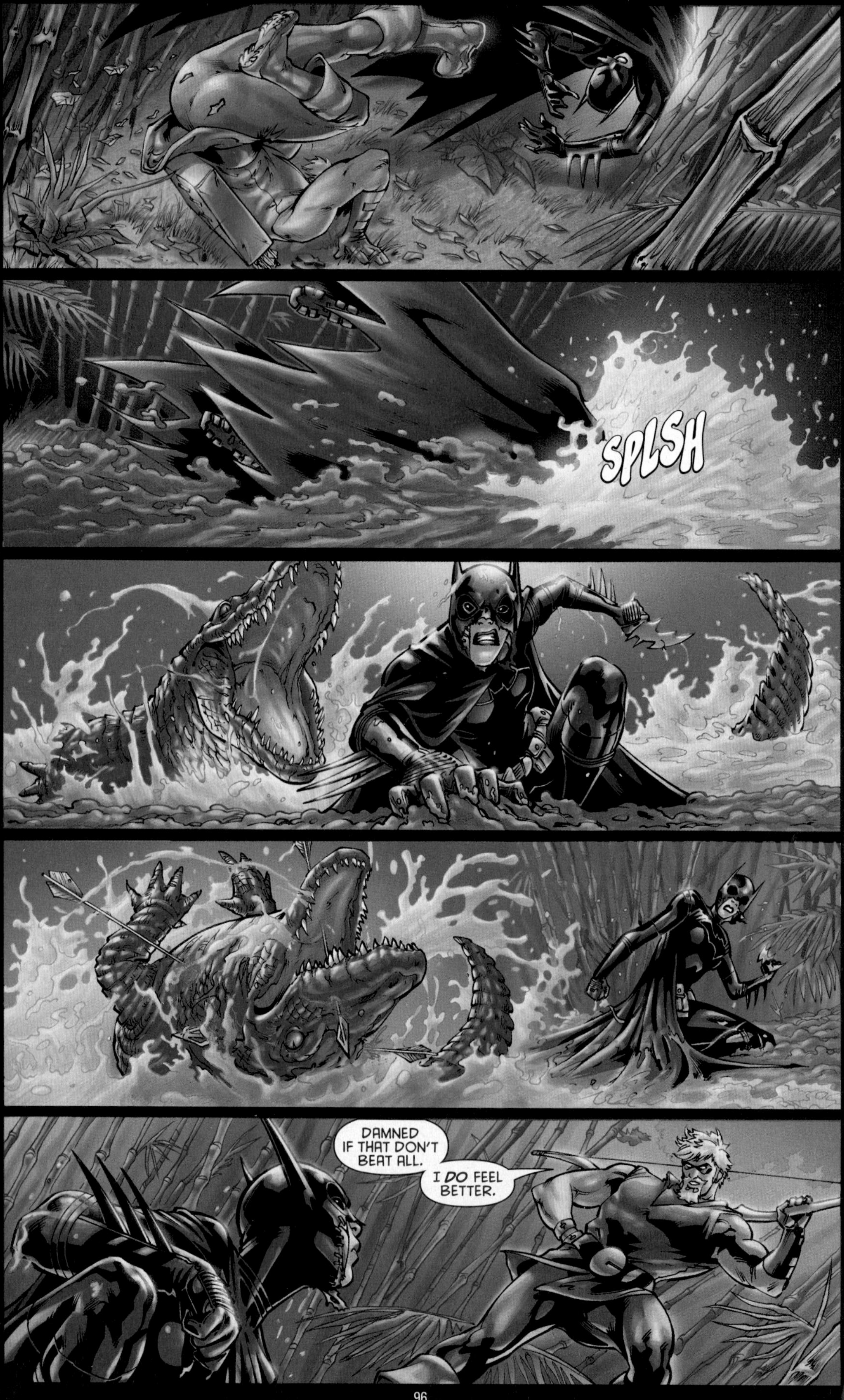
SPLSH
DAMNED IF THAT DON'T BEAT ALL.
I *DO* FEEL BETTER.

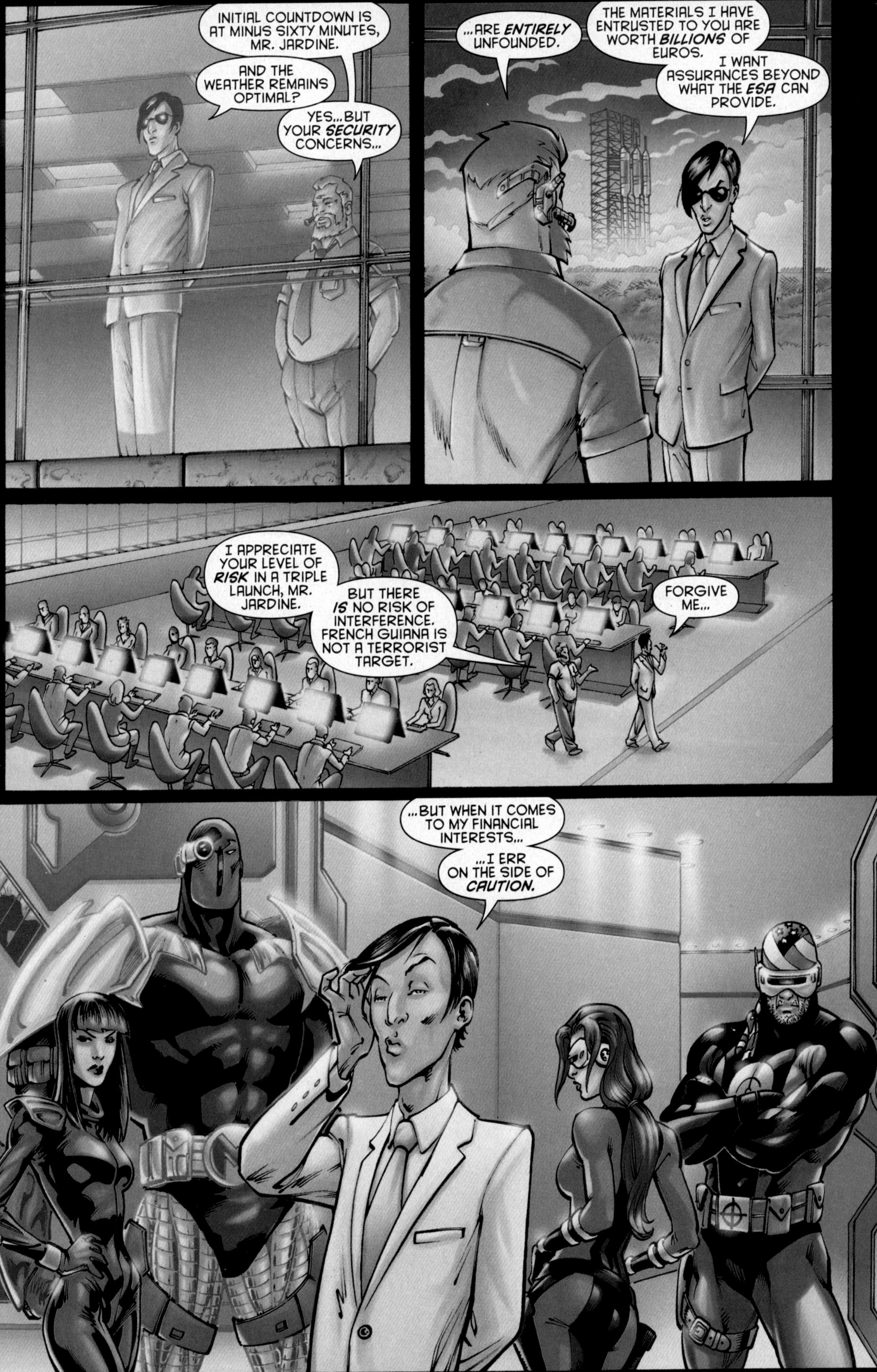
INITIAL COUNTDOWN IS AT MINUS SIXTY MINUTES, MR. JARDINE.
AND THE WEATHER REMAINS OPTIMAL?
YES...BUT YOUR SECURITY CONCERNS...
...ARE ENTIRELY UNFOUNDED.
THE MATERIALS I HAVE ENTRUSTED TO YOU ARE WORTH BILLIONS OF EUROS.
I WANT ASSURANCES BEYOND WHAT THE ESA CAN PROVIDE.
I APPRECIATE YOUR LEVEL OF RISK IN A TRIPLE LAUNCH, MR. JARDINE.
BUT THERE IS NO RISK OF INTERFERENCE. FRENCH GUIANA IS NOT A TERRORIST TARGET.
FORGIVE ME...
...BUT WHEN IT COMES TO MY FINANCIAL INTERESTS...
...I ERR ON THE SIDE OF CAUTION.

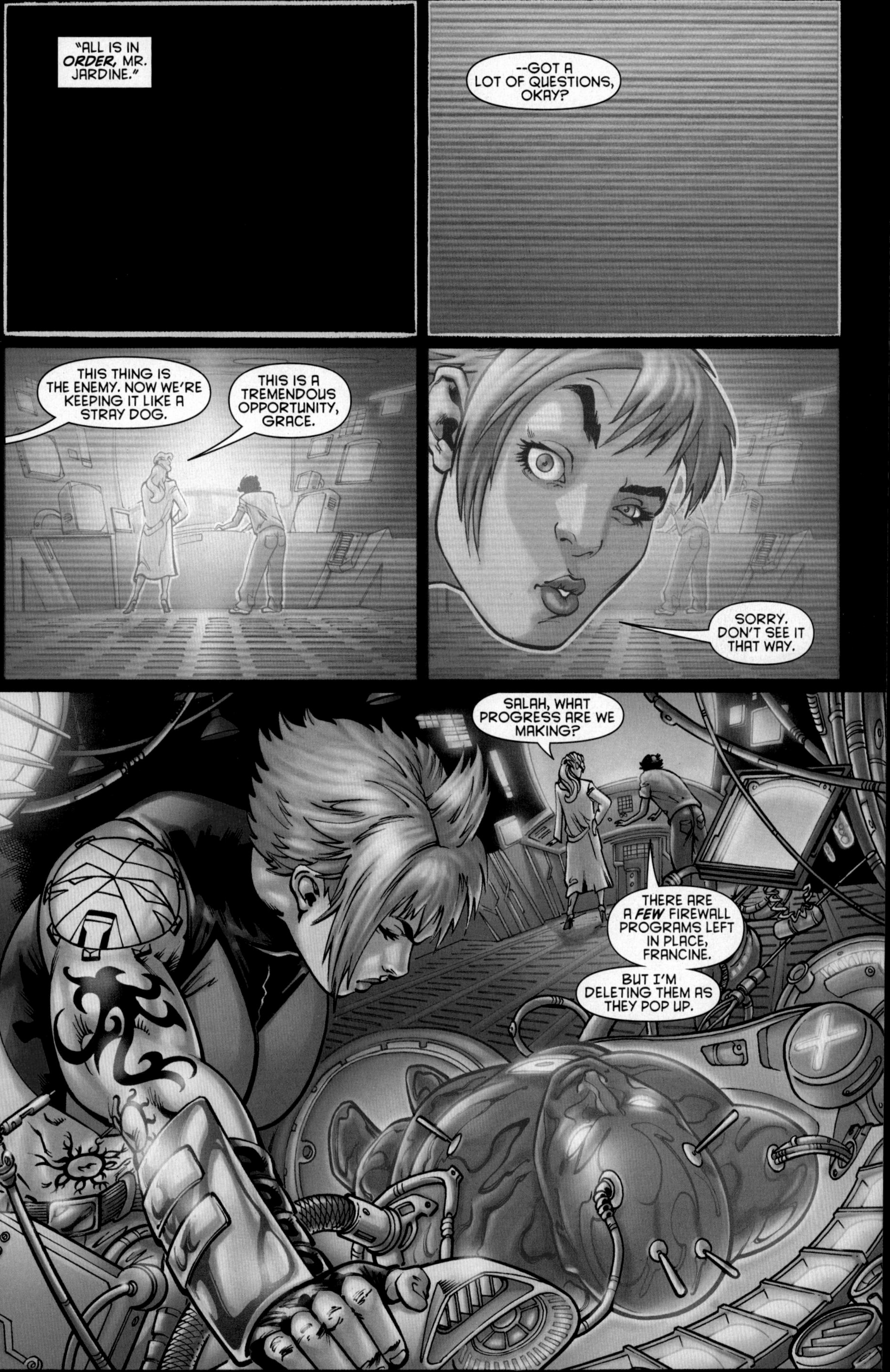
"ALL IS IN ORDER, MR. JARDINE."
--GOT A LOT OF QUESTIONS, OKAY?
THIS THING IS THE ENEMY. NOW WE'RE KEEPING IT LIKE A STRAY DOG.
THIS IS A TREMENDOUS OPPORTUNITY, GRACE.
SORRY. DON'T SEE IT THAT WAY.
SALAH, WHAT PROGRESS ARE WE MAKING?
THERE ARE A FEW FIREWALL PROGRAMS LEFT IN PLACE, FRANCINE.
BUT I'M DELETING THEM AS THEY POP UP.

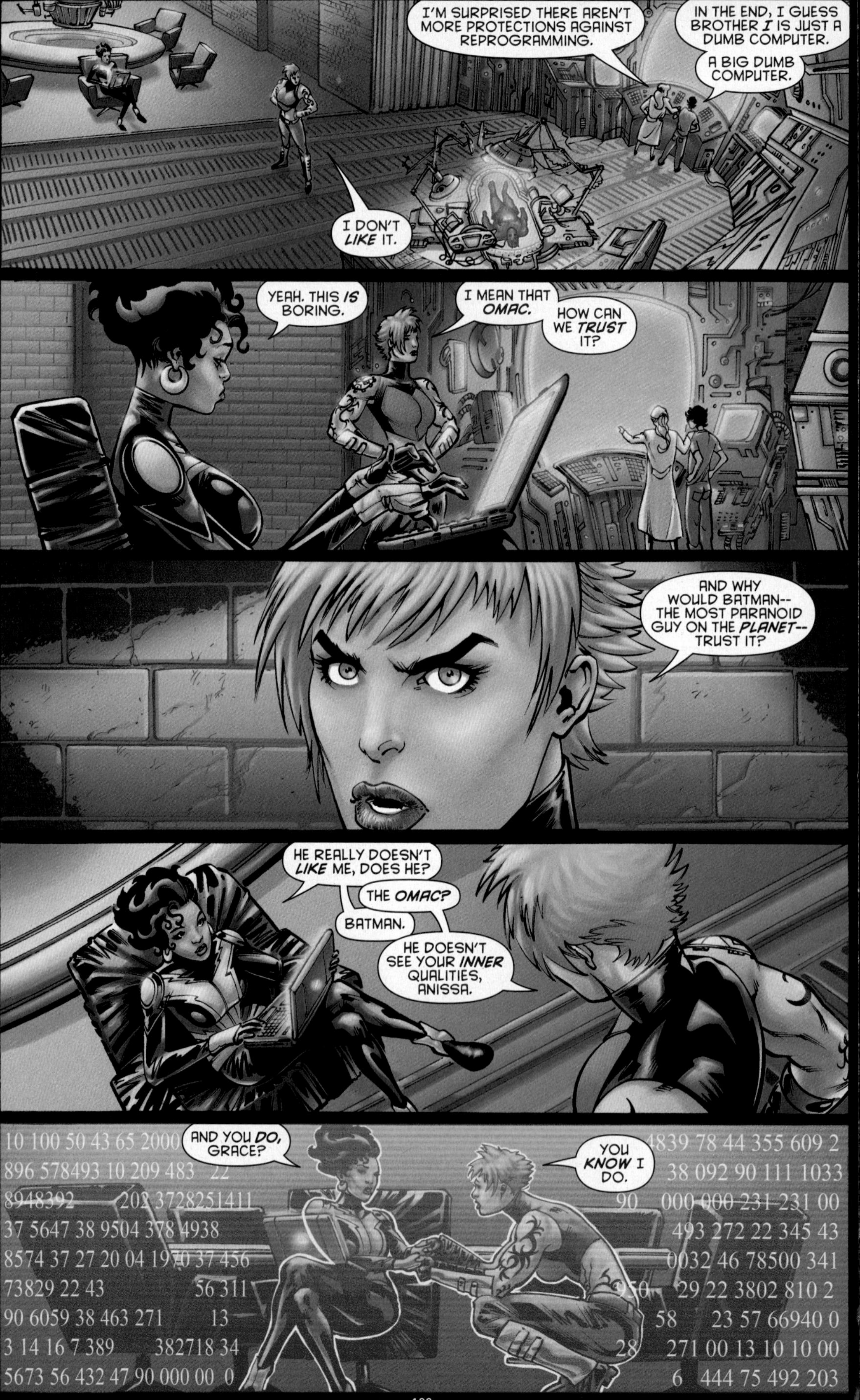
I'M SURPRISED THERE AREN'T MORE PROTECTIONS AGAINST REPROGRAMMING.
IN THE END, I GUESS BROTHER *I* IS JUST A DUMB COMPUTER.
A BIG DUMB COMPUTER.
I DON'T *LIKE* IT.
YEAH. THIS *IS* BORING.
I MEAN THAT *OMAC.*
HOW CAN WE *TRUST* IT?
AND WHY WOULD BATMAN-- THE MOST PARANOID GUY ON THE *PLANET*-- TRUST IT?
HE REALLY DOESN'T *LIKE* ME, DOES HE?
THE *OMAC?*
BATMAN.
HE DOESN'T SEE YOUR *INNER* QUALITIES, ANISSA.
AND YOU *DO,* GRACE?
YOU *KNOW* I DO.

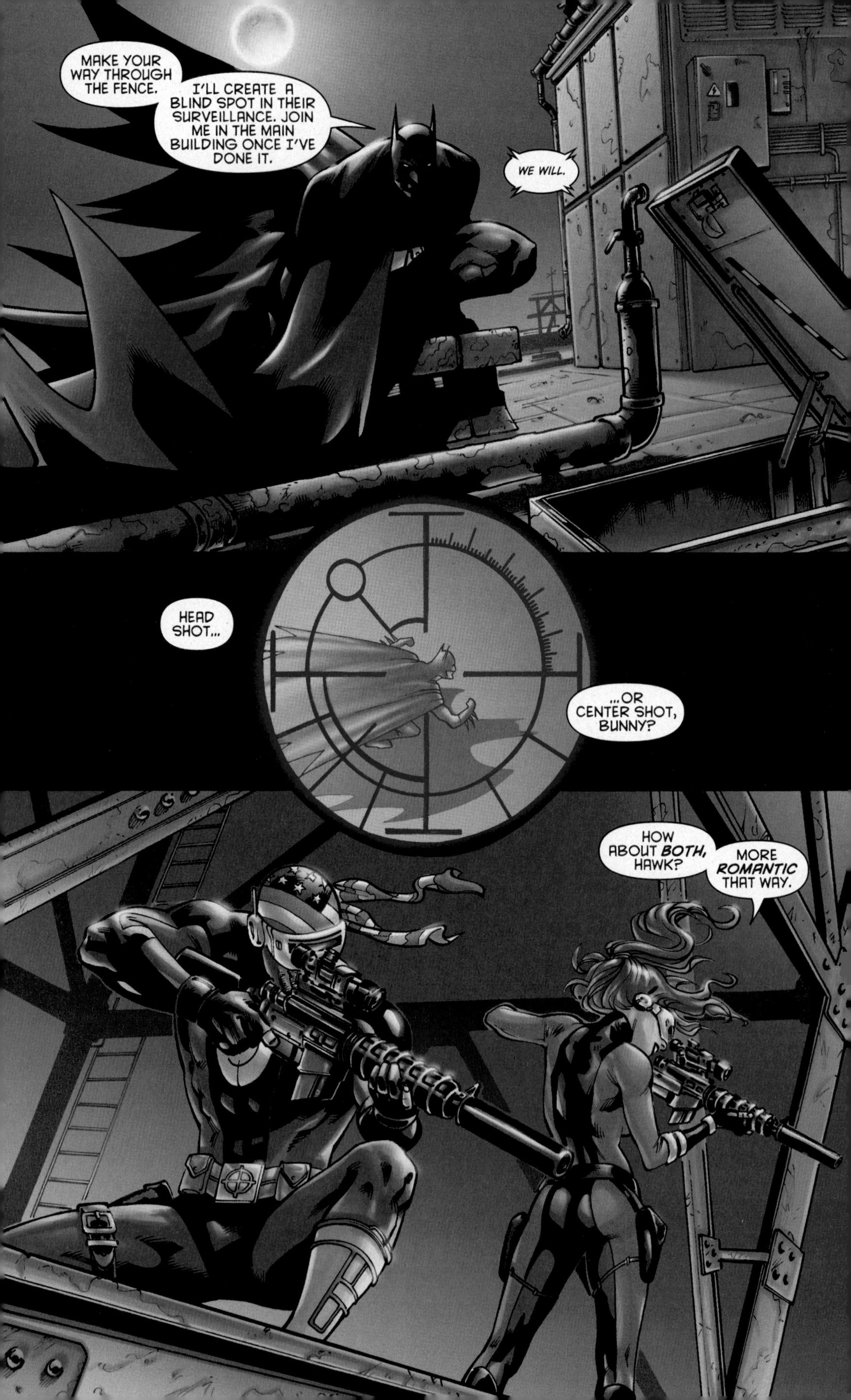
MAKE YOUR WAY THROUGH THE FENCE.
I'LL CREATE A BLIND SPOT IN THEIR SURVEILLANCE. JOIN ME IN THE MAIN BUILDING ONCE I'VE DONE IT.
WE WILL.
HEAD SHOT...
...OR CENTER SHOT, BUNNY?
HOW ABOUT BOTH, HAWK?
MORE ROMANTIC THAT WAY.

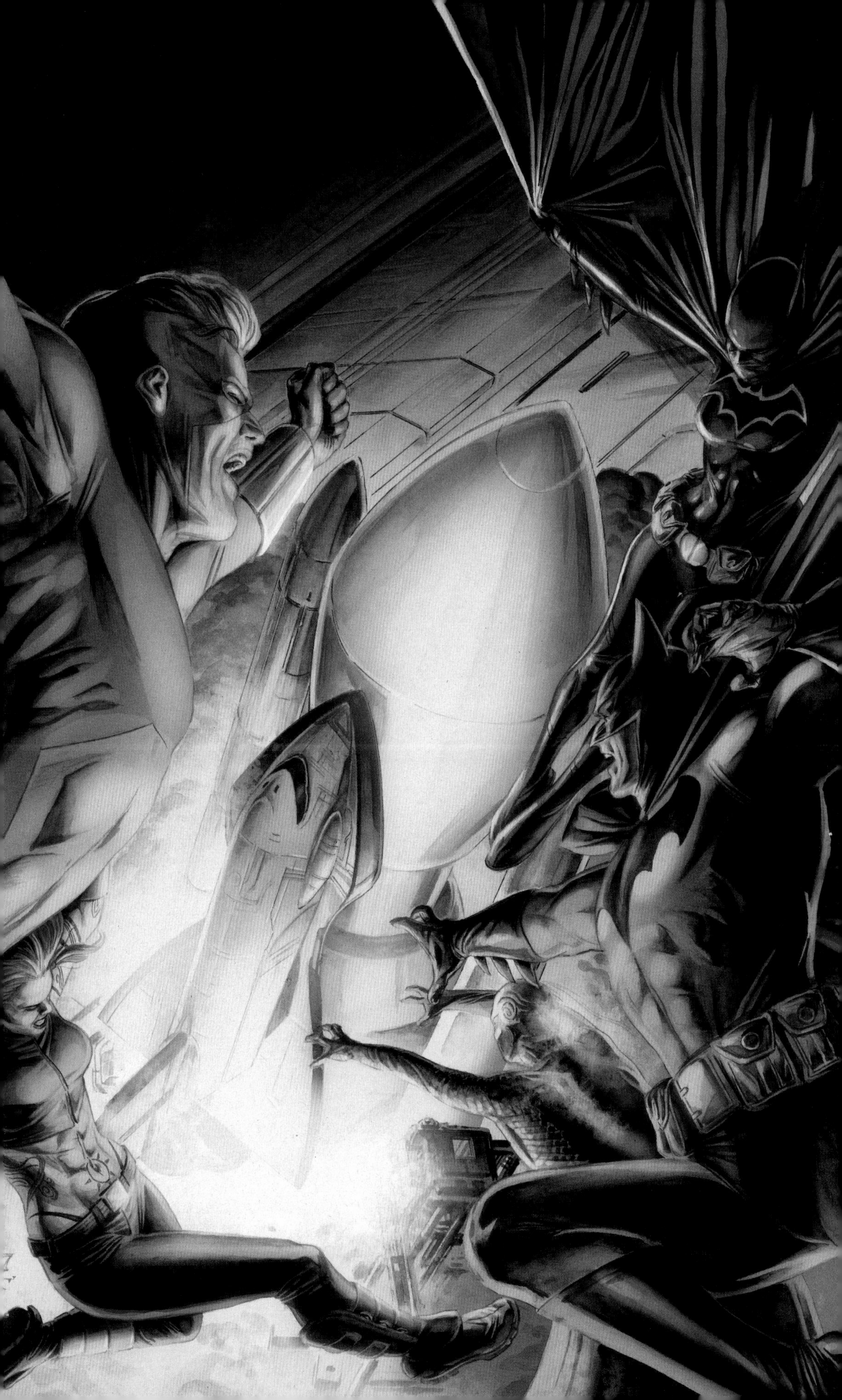

part FIVE

Uh!

Hunh!

Batgirl

Metamorpho

Katana

LET'S *HUSTLE,* FOLKS! NO TELLING HOW LONG THIS BLIND SPOT WILL HOLD.

REX, GET US INSIDE.

IT'S WHAT I *DO,* OLLIE.

BUT I DON'T REMEMBER BATMAN MAKING YOU *EL JEFE.*

WE'LL TAKE IT UP AT THE NEXT MEETING, OKAY?

I'LL BRING THE SANDWICHES.

--YOU'RE STILL A *NEWBIE.*

AS FAR AS THE OUTSIDERS ARE CONCERNED--

KEEP OUT

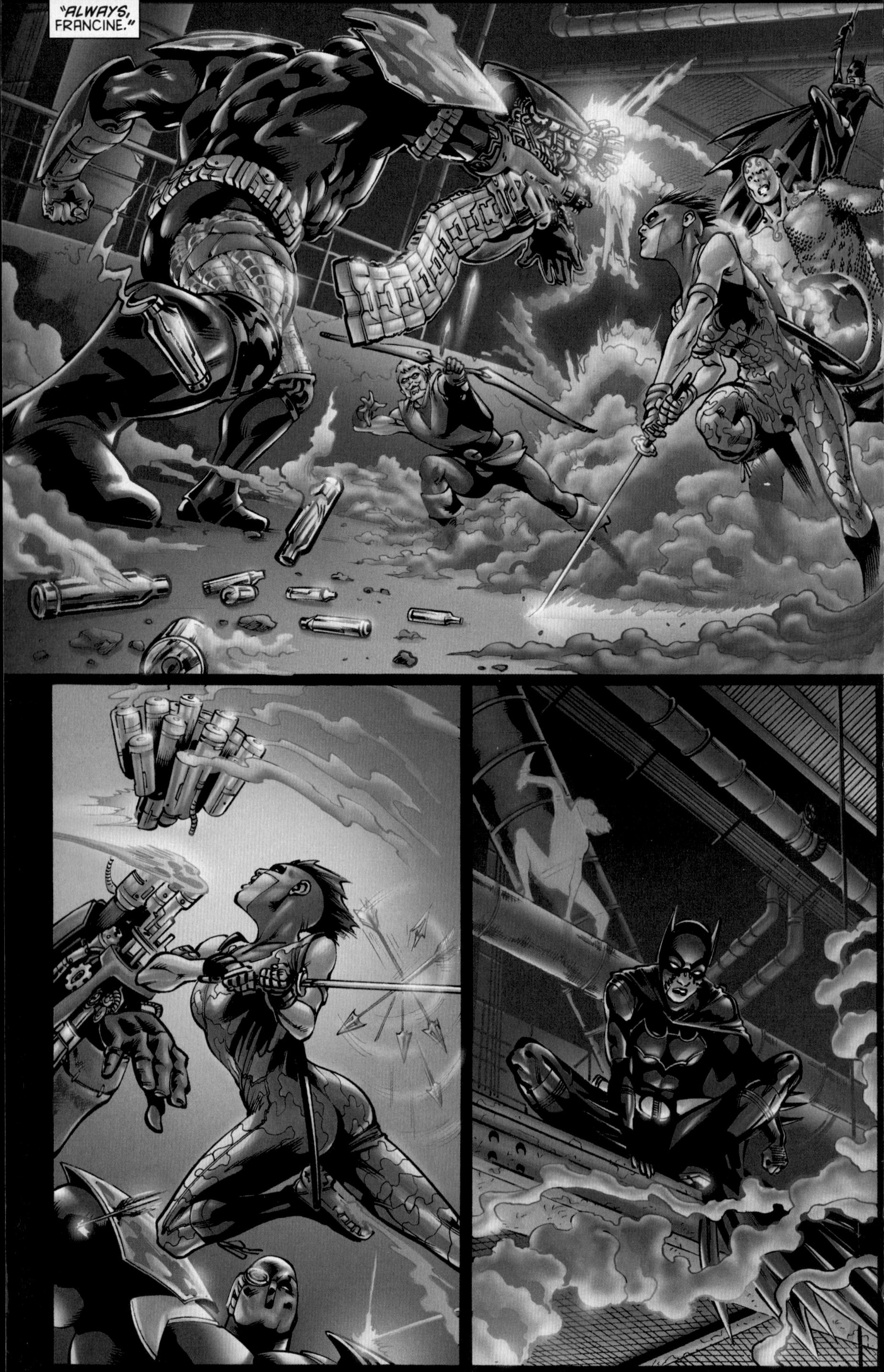
"ALWAYS, FRANCINE."

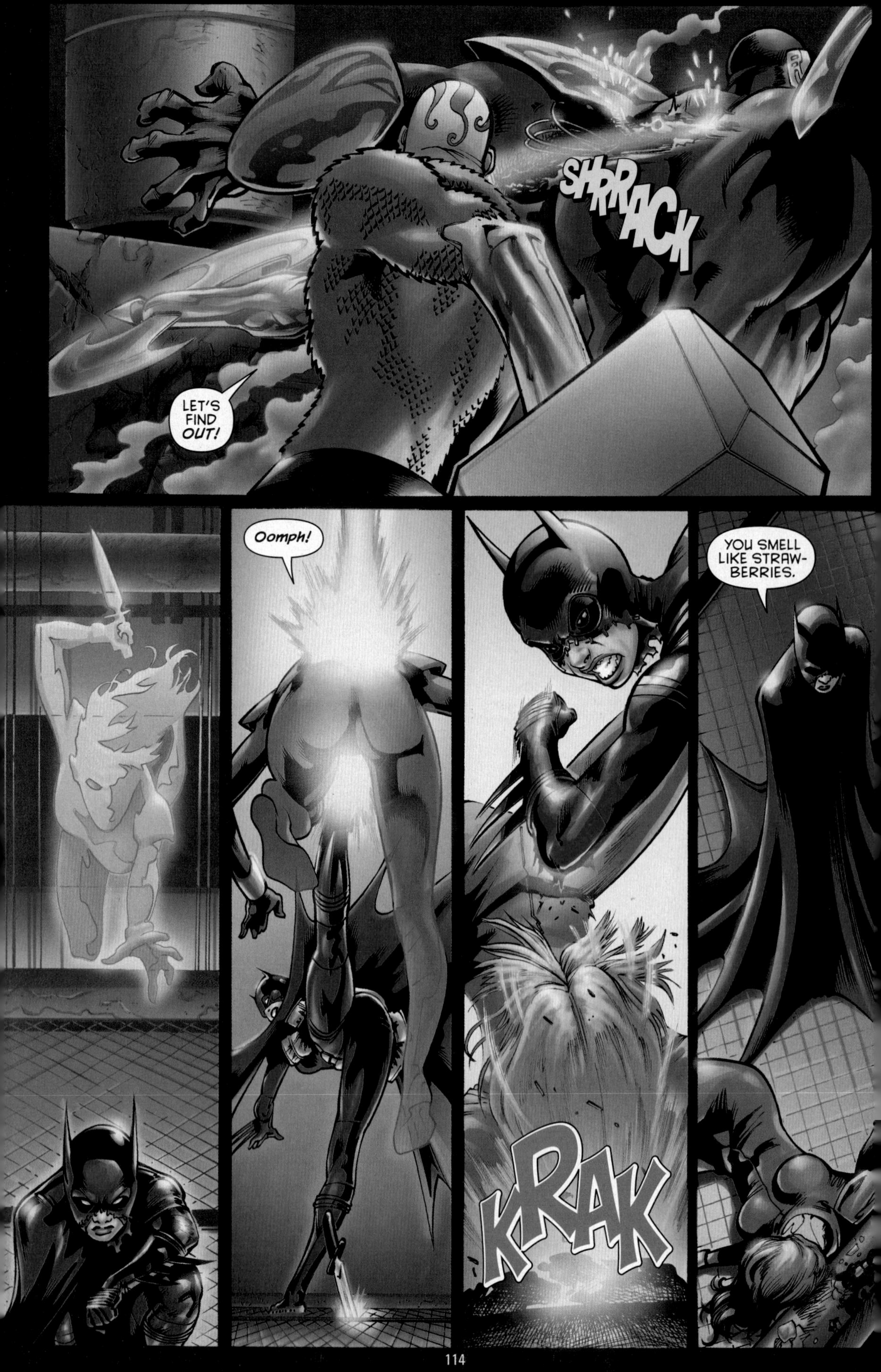
SHRRACK
LET'S FIND OUT!
Oomph!
KRAK
YOU SMELL LIKE STRAW-BERRIES.

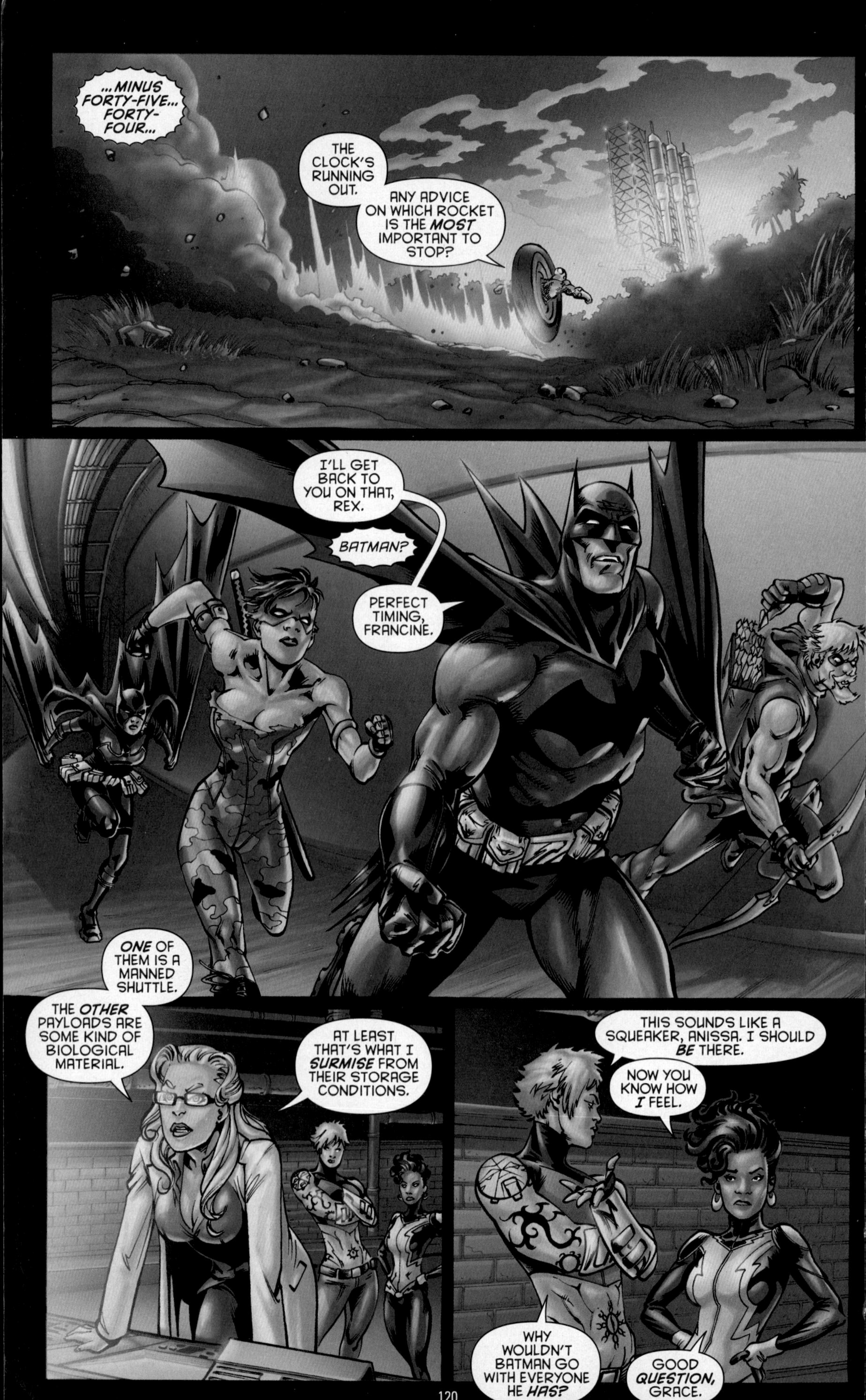
...MINUS FORTY-FIVE... FORTY-FOUR...
THE CLOCK'S RUNNING OUT.
ANY ADVICE ON WHICH ROCKET IS THE *MOST* IMPORTANT TO STOP?
I'LL GET BACK TO YOU ON THAT, REX.
BATMAN?
PERFECT TIMING, FRANCINE.
ONE OF THEM IS A MANNED SHUTTLE.
THE *OTHER* PAYLOADS ARE SOME KIND OF BIOLOGICAL MATERIAL.
AT LEAST THAT'S WHAT I *SURMISE* FROM THEIR STORAGE CONDITIONS.
THIS SOUNDS LIKE A SQUEAKER, ANISSA. I SHOULD *BE* THERE.
NOW YOU KNOW HOW *I* FEEL.
WHY WOULDN'T BATMAN GO WITH EVERYONE HE *HAS?*
GOOD *QUESTION,* GRACE.

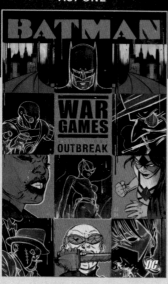